COULD YOU SURVIVE SHARK TANK?

Aaron,

Thank you for lending the way!

God Bless you!

Piim Mann

The Sharks' **Top 7 Questions Every Entrepreneur Must Answer**

COULD YOU SURVIVE SHARK TANK?

WRITTEN BY THE HOST OF THE SHARK TANK FAN PODCAST

PIERCE MARRS

AND CONTRIBUTING AUTHORS

INCLUDES INTERVIEW WITH SCRUB DADDY® FOUNDER, AARON KRAUSE

4mpress

Thompson's Station, TN

© 2020 by Pierce Marrs

Published by 4mpress
PO Box 134
Thompson's Station, TN 37179

All rights reserved. No portion of this book may be reproduced, stored in a retrieval system, or transmitted in any form or by any means—electronic, mechanical, photocopy, recording, scanning, or other—except for brief quotations in critical reviews or articles, without the prior written permission of the publisher.

Scripture quotations are taken from THE HOLY BIBLE, NEW INTERNATIONAL VERSION®, NIV® Copyright © 1973, 1978, 1984, 2011 by Biblica, Inc.® Used by permission. All rights reserved worldwide.

Cover Design by Jimi Gibson; Jimigibson.com
Edited by Amanda Price, Right Price Editing
Interior Layout and eBook by LParnell Book Services

ISBN: 978-0-9896681-1-8 (Print)

ISBN: 978-0-9896681-2-5 (eBook)

Printed in the United States of America

DEDICATION

*To all who believe
the American dream is alive and well.*

Contents

Introduction: The Allure of *Shark Tank* 1

Chapter 1. Are You an Entrepreneur? 5
Chapter 2. The List 9
Chapter 3. The Right Questions 11
Chapter 4. *Question One:*
 "Do You Have Any Sales?" 23
Chapter 5. *Question Two: "How Did You Come Up*
 with That Valuation?" 39
Chapter 6. *Question Three: "How Did You Finance*
 Your Business?" 53
Chapter 7. *Question Four: "Do You Want or Need*
 a Partner?" 65
Chapter 8. *Question Five: "Do You Have a Patent?"* 77
Chapter 9. *Question Six: "Is Your Product*
 or Company a Brand?" 85
Chapter 10. *Question Seven: "What Is Your Plan?"* 99

Contents

Chapter 11. *Bonus Question:* "Should Your Business Give Back?" 109
Chapter 12. Summary 113

Acknowledgments 117
Notes 119
About the Author 125

INTRODUCTION

The Allure of *Shark Tank*

In August of 2009, a new show aired on American TV that allowed hopeful entrepreneurs to stand before a panel of wealthy businesspeople and make a pitch for an investment in their business. It was called *Shark Tank*, and I was immediately hooked.

As a lifetime sales professional, entrepreneur, and business coach, I was intrigued by the entire process—the presentation of a new idea, the sales pitch, and the negotiation. I listened closely to the advice the Sharks were offering and the reason for investing or not investing in a certain company.

I called my lifelong friend Steve Hayes to talk about each episode of the first season. This felt natural for us since we had been having these same conversations for years before *Shark Tank* existed. We were both very interested in new business ideas, products, inventions, and the new ways people were approaching entrepreneurship. We discussed in depth the quality of presentations, what they did wrong or right. We asked ourselves if the product was viable. Would we buy it? Did the Sharks make the correct decision to invest or pass?

At some point during that first season, I decided this would be a great premise for a podcast. It was logical for me to talk about sales and communication since I had spent my entire business life studying and practicing those skills. I had also spent the last several years coaching individuals and businesses on these same topics. *Shark Tank* encompassed all of this in one neat package. I called Steve to be my cohost, and we were ready to get started.

In April of 2011, we aired our first episode of the *Shark Tank Fan Podcast,* where we recap each episode and discuss the quality of the presentation, the viability of the products, and the reactions from the Sharks. We have also been fortunate to interview many of the entrepreneurs who have appeared on the show, along with a couple of Sharks.

It has long been my desire to write a book about *Shark Tank* for fans and hopeful entrepreneurs alike. For those who watch the show for the mere entertainment, I hope this book will give you a better understanding of the terminology and discussions taking place on the show. If you are building your own business and would love the opportunity to present on *Shark Tank*, I hope this book will help you move faster and understand the steps required to prepare for that opportunity.

Unfortunately, the opportunity to gain valuable exposure in front of millions of viewers on *Shark Tank* has become a lottery, with thousands of applicants and only a handful making the final cut. I hope you have the vision and courage to ask yourself the same questions that the Sharks would ask if you were standing before them. The answers to those questions could be the catalyst to take your business to the next level. I hope this book will be a guide to help you avoid many of the stumbling blocks that hinder you from reaching your

The Allure of Shark Tank

goals. Wherever you are right now, you are swimming in your own *Shark Tank*, and I want to help you not only survive but thrive in your business.

Growing your business is difficult to do on your own. None of us have the expertise and time to do everything our business requires by ourselves. We have to engage with people who possess talents and strengths that we do not. When I laid out the plan for this book, I realized quickly that I was not qualified to speak as an expert about all the topics covered. I sought the expertise of several successful people who lent their wisdom and insight to this project, and I am very grateful. You will receive the benefit of hearing from these successful entrepreneurs, who include a *New York Times* best-selling author, a CEO, a former attorney, a marketing and branding expert, and the owner of the most successful business to come out of *Shark Tank*.

Shark Tank is wildly popular with people of all ages and has rekindled the American dream for many hopeful entrepreneurs. Join me and some of the smartest people I know as we help you win in your own *Shark Tank*.

CHAPTER 1

Are You an Entrepreneur?

If you are reading this, you are most likely a fan of *Shark Tank*, an entrepreneur, or dream of being an entrepreneur.

Merriam-Webster defines an entrepreneur as "one who organizes, manages, and assumes the risks of a business or enterprise."[1]

Over the past ten seasons, *Shark Tank* has proven that entrepreneurs come in all types. All of the individuals who stand before the Sharks have different personalities, strengths, challenges, backgrounds, and education.

The Small Business Administration stated in their 2019 Small Business Profile that there are 30.7 million small businesses in the United States making up 99.9 percent of all businesses. They qualify a small business as an independent business having fewer than five hundred employees.[2]

Firms with less than one hundred employees have the largest share of business employment.

When someone mentions successful businesses, it is easy to think of companies like Apple, Amazon, and Google. While they employ thousands of people, in reality, these mammoth businesses make up a small percentage of business in America.

Small business is the backbone of our economy, and it has been a joy for me to spend the last several years working with entrepreneurs and their teams to help them accomplish their objectives and reach new levels of success.

> *Not everyone is going to understand everything about business, but you have to be honest with yourself and self aware about what you don't know.*
> —MARK CUBAN[3]

As a business coach and strategic team builder, I have realized that every person who owns a business or manages a team comes to the table with their own personality and unique set of skills, opportunities, and challenges. The people who are sufficiently self-aware of these strengths and challenges have the greatest potential for growth.

I am sure we can agree all reality shows are edited and presented in a way to provide the most entertainment and generate the highest ratings for their network. *Shark Tank* is no different.

So, what is real? The entrepreneurs on *Shark Tank* are real people with real ideas and businesses. The Sharks are real millionaires and billionaires using their own money to invest. The Sharks have to ask a lot of questions to make a quick decision to invest. The due diligence can take several months after the deal is made, resulting in a percentage of the deals never making it to contract. Bottom line—in the eleven seasons *Shark Tank* has been on the air, millions of dollars have been invested, and a lot of lives have been changed. That's real!

Over the years, I have coached individuals and teams struggling with the same issues that have made you cringe while watching an entrepreneur melt down during a *Shark Tank* segment. I want to help you avoid those moments.

In the following pages, I have attempted to make you aware of many of the questions that require your attention to be a successful entrepreneur. It is my hope that while creating answers to these questions, your dream of entrepreneurship will transform into a viable, profitable business.

CHAPTER 2

The List

Barbara Corcoran stated in an interview that one of her most successful investments, Cousins Maine Lobster, which appeared on *Shark Tank* in 2012, watched every episode and prepared answers to every question. The result was a well-executed presentation that garnered them a deal with Barbara in spite of the fact that they had been in business a short time.

Much can be learned from these young entrepreneurs. Undoubtedly, their preparation for the show forced Sabin Lomac and Jim Tselikis to look closely at their business and make critical decisions on how to answer them. As a result, they presented a more complete business outlook that made it much easier for Barbara to take the plunge and invest.

As I considered the genius of their preparation, I asked myself, "What if every entrepreneur, even if they never appeared on *Shark Tank*, conducted this same exercise with his or her own business?"

After recording over 180 podcast episodes, recapping ten of the eleven seasons of *Shark Tank*, and interviewing multiple entrepreneurs and Sharks from the show, I have learned that the millionaires and billionaires on the panel will probe to get the information they need. They want to know if they invest in your business, whether they can get their money back and make a profit.

Inspired by this article, I began to generate an exhaustive list of the questions the Sharks have asked over the years. The list was long, but after a while, I saw a trend. Many of the questions were asking the same information, just stated differently. Almost all of the questions fell into seven different categories. Each category had a subset of questions that delved deeper into that particular subject.

Though the questions are similar, the answers vary for each person, product, and business. Every entrepreneur and business has a unique personality and should choose their path accordingly. It would be foolish to propose the same strategic plan for every business that comes into the Tank.

The Sharks are investing their own money. This is not play money! They have a personal interest to invest in businesses that will yield the greatest return. Each Shark may look for different attributes in entrepreneurs, ranging from the products to the business plan, but they all have the same end game—what's in it for me?

If these wealthy investors are asking questions to find out if a business has a chance of a profitable return, shouldn't you be asking yourself those same questions?

Barbara Corcoran took a chance on Cousins Maine Lobster. Seven years after being on *Shark Tank*, they have surpassed fifty million in sales. They took the importance of *questions* seriously, and so should you.

CHAPTER 3

The Right Questions

For That Reason I'm Out: Moose Head Kettle Corn

Jack contacted me and asked if we could meet as soon as possible. His demeanor was a mix of excitement and concern. He shared briefly what he wanted to discuss, and we scheduled a meeting. As we sat across from each other, he shared with me the details of their business. They were doing well and he was enjoying their success, but he had to make a decision.

A friend told them they should apply to be on *Shark Tank*, and on a whim, they filled out the application and sent it in. They did not believe they had a chance of getting selected due to the popularity of the show and the large number of applicants who wanted their shot to present their business to the Sharks.

They were wrong. The producers were very interested in having Jack and Carol MacDowall on the show to pitch for an investment in their business, Moose Head Kettle Corn.

Carol conducted the phone interview, and it went very well. Next, they received the contract to review, sign, and return. Then it would be time to video.

Jack called me when he received the contract. He was apprehensive. Their kettle corn business was going well. They worked the business as a family, selling their product at the Tennessee Titans football games, the Grand Ole Opry, Nashville Farmers Market, and various festivals and events across the country. They had grown their enterprise into a six-figure company and were debt free.

> *Remember that the quality of your answers is going to be determined by the quality of your questions.*
> —ANDY ANDREWS

"I just don't know if I want to give up part of my company," he stated soberly.

We discussed the pros and cons of being on the show and what an investment from the Sharks would do for his business. How would he handle the increased sales if he did appear on an episode? Could he keep up with the demand? Would it change the way he produced his product? Did he want more employees? Ultimately, he was not only concerned with his business but also the kind of life he wanted for his family.

After a long discussion, it was clear that Jack and Carol would not pursue an appearance on *Shark Tank*. They were happy with their business as it was at the time. They knew their business and had planned well. All of the opportunities that a *Shark Tank* appearance would bring did not align with the future goals for their company and family.

Jack and Carol were willing to ask themselves some hard questions and had the courage to follow through.

Every business, regardless of where it is right now, should ask many of the same questions that the savvy investors on

Shark Tank ask each contestant when they stand before them. Have you asked yourself those questions? Have you thought about what you would say when challenged to explain why your company is worth an investment?

These are not always easy questions to answer, but they are vital to the success of your business. The right questions can give you clarity on how you want to position yourself in the market, who your ideal customer is, and if this particular business model lines up with your personality, talents, and abilities.

Moose Head Kettle Corn survived their *Shark Tank* because they knew themselves and their business well enough to make the best decisions for both.

The Power of Questions

Google ran a brilliant advertisement that began with a white screen, and then these words appeared:

> *A question …*
>
> *A question is the most powerful force in the world …*
>
> *A question … can take you anywhere."*

As I write these words, *Shark Tank* is well into season eleven. It has aired two-hundred plus episodes, with hundreds of pitches, and the Sharks have invested millions of dollars and asked *thousands of questions.*

After watching a few episodes, it doesn't take long to see a trend in the types of questions being asked. If you stop for a moment and close your eyes, you can probably hear Mr. Wonderful asking, "Tell us about your sales." You may have slapped your forehead in frustration at someone who doesn't know their numbers, not to mention those outrageous valuations!

I love new ideas, and I can't wait to hear the pitch and find out how someone has created something new or improved on an existing idea. However, the questions during the negotiation will make or break you.

A few years ago, I had the opportunity to sit in on a mock *Shark Tank* panel. We listened to pitches and began to ask entrepreneurs about their business to help them find direction and clarity.

Several of the participants became uncomfortable quickly. The process was uncovering exactly where they were in their business, and for some it was shocking. In that moment, it occurred to me that these hopeful entrepreneurs, or as Mark Cuban calls them, the *wantrepreneurs*, had never asked themselves the hard questions.

The Hard Parts

Marketing Guru Seth Godin wrote in his blog *The Hard Parts*, "If you can't describe the hard parts, how will you focus on them?" He goes on to say that when he meets an entrepreneur, he always asks this question first, "Which part of your project is hard?"[1]

The tricky part about identifying the hard parts is that it is different for each person and each project. Our personality, talent, knowledge, and life experience play a part in the easy and the hard stuff. What may be easy for you may be difficult for me and vice versa.

The one thing you can count on is that if you want to do anything worthwhile and create change, there will be hard parts. It doesn't matter if you want to own your own business, be a successful salesperson, invent and market a new idea, write a book, or be a better spouse or parent. There will be times when you will have to ask yourself some hard questions.

One of my best friends took Godin's advice. While Jason Cruise was finalizing the business plan for his new venture, he sat down with nine of the most successful, trustworthy people he knew and asked the hardest question: "Tell me why this will fail."

I'm sure my friend wanted to hear how great an idea he had, but he knew by asking them to identify the weaknesses, he would give himself a greater chance of success and avoid unnecessary pitfalls.

> *Plans fail for lack of counsel, but with many advisers they succeed.*
> —PROVERBS 15:22 (NIV)

Many *Shark Tank* presenters come on the show emotionally attached to their idea and reject the notion that it might not work. They leave the tank more determined than ever to prove the Sharks wrong. The entrepreneurs who generate the greatest success after *Shark Tank* carefully consider the counsel they receive from the Sharks and implement that advice into their business.

Hard questions can challenge you and be uncomfortable. However, a lot of people are willing to do the easy stuff and settle for mediocrity. If you are willing to grow and face the hard stuff, you can stand out from the crowd and see uncommon success.

Asking the Right Questions

Entrepreneur and Tesla founder Elon Musk was asked in an *Inc. Magazine* interview the one creative skill he'd suggest you learn to be the best founder you can be. "Chances are, it's how to ask the right question," Musk believes. "A lot of times the question is harder than the answer. If you can properly phrase the question, then the answer is the easy part."[2]

Asking the right questions can be pivotal to your success by broadening your perspective and helping you make smarter decisions. Asking the wrong questions can leave you defeated and prepared to give up. For example, "Why does this always happen to me?" or "What did I do to deserve this?" The answers to these questions are not productive and do not produce positive results. Instead, ask yourself, "What does this experience make possible? What can I do to prevent this from happening again? What can I learn from this experience that will help me in the future?"

> *We make our world significant by the courage of our questions and by the depth of our answers.*
> —CARL SAGAN

Each time I have had the opportunity to coach an entrepreneur, the session always begins with a lot of questions. Specifically, it involves knowing the right questions to ask and gaining a new perspective. Most people have the answers inside them. They just need another person to draw them out and bring clarity to their direction.

I encounter a lot of people who are creative and come up with multiple ideas, but they never seem to get traction. Recently I met with Robert, who was frustrated and wanted to increase his income. He shared several of his ideas, and I realized he was a very creative person but did not have a plan. He had taken a couple of his ideas to the prototype stage but no further. One in particular had been created six years before our meeting. When he first came up with this idea, he was challenged by a friend who loved the idea and agreed to help Robert sell the product but goodheartedly advised that he should be prepared to fill the orders.

The Right Questions

After I met with Robert and discussing the logistics to get his product to market, things began to happen. He wrote down the actual steps that would have to be taken to move forward with his idea. This activity made him look at his business in a new light. He started seeing the challenges of scaling and creating enough momentum to create an income. When he asked himself some hard questions and examined the facts, a new perspective of his business began to emerge. He decided to shelve this product and apply the same process to his next best idea.

Asking the proper questions is vital to the launch and growth of your business. The answers may become difficult and challenge you, but the process will also help you evaluate the viability of your product or service and help you discover obstacles early so you can overcome them or abort a specific plan of action before it is too late.

Whether growing a business, improving your health, or having a more productive life, it all comes down to asking the *right* questions and having the courage to answer them honestly.

Shark Inquisition

As entrepreneurs step confidently down the hallway beside the CG shark tanks and stand before those five Sharks, they must be prepared to answer multiple questions. The Sharks take an average of sixty to ninety minutes to learn all they can about a business to determine if it is a viable investment. As viewers, we see a few minutes of the total time an entrepreneur spends in the tank. In a nutshell, all of the questions outlined in this book are designed to give the Sharks answers to the following questions:

1. What is the current status of your business?
2. What direction do you want to take your business?
3. What is your plan to get there?

If you are prepared and deliver well-thought-out answers, there is a good chance that one or more of the Sharks will be ready to invest and partner with you in your business. What if you never make it on *Shark Tank*? More than ever, your business is demanding that you answer the same questions.

Just like most great questions, these three questions breed more questions and force you to go deeper. This process allows you to examine your business more closely and proactively anticipate issues before they arise. Either you have the answers or you don't. Regardless, you now have the ability to deal with the issues that arise appropriately without getting blindsided. Some of my favorites pitches left *Shark Tank* without a deal, heeded the advice of the Sharks, and went on to create a successful business, including Chef Big Shake, CoatChex, and Proof Eyewear, to name a few.

Besides the tremendous exposure of being seen by millions of viewers, getting to spend time with a panel of millionaires and billionaires can be priceless if you keep an open mind and open ears. For us as fans and observers, we can enjoy the show and gain valuable insight as well.

Having the knowledge of your business and a vision of where you want it to go is vital to creating an effective game plan. We will discuss this topic in chapter ten.

The following is a case study of an actual client who was faced with these questions and how she responded.

Ecodiva

In February 2016, I was one of three speakers who was scheduled to speak to a room full of high school entrepreneurs. The first speaker was a fireball who had created her own line of toxin-free personal care products, including sunscreen, bug spray, and even a doggy wash. She projected a contagious enthusiasm about entrepreneurship and her business, Ecodiva.

After the event, I had the pleasure of meeting Jody Norcio and hearing more of her story. She had done what some people only hope to accomplish. She had an idea, gave it legs, and created her own business from nothing but a dream.

During the conversation, she voiced some concerns and roadblocks she was experiencing in her business and asked if I would consider being her coach. After a more in-depth discussion, I agreed.

In our first session, Jody stated emphatically that she wanted to build her business so she could sell it. What began as a dream had turned into a drain physically and emotionally. At the time, she was selling her products online, at farmers markets, and through a few local boutiques and had successfully acquired shelf space in over forty Kroger stores.

From the outside, everything looked great. She had created a high-quality product with a clever name that signified her brand, and most importantly, her customers loved the product and kept coming back for more. Sounds great, right?

Behind the scenes, Jody was working tirelessly to fulfill all of the roles of a small company. She was the salesperson, wholesale broker, demo girl at Kroger, accountant, and in charge of mixing each bottle of every product in her basement.

It was beginning to affect her health, and she was tired.

We started by breaking down all the pieces of her business and the steps required to bring a product to market. Then we discussed the items that could and should be delegated.

One of the most glaring issues we faced was trying to figure how much profit she was making. Jody was doing a reasonable job of keeping her books. She knew the costs of her product and her wholesale and retail pricing like the back of her hand, but it was difficult to pin down specific information about profitability and specifically where that profit was coming from.

This was a key in finding how to develop her business and make it attractive to a potential buyer.

Michael Gerber, author of the best-selling book *The E-Myth*, is famous for reminding entrepreneurs to work on their business and not in it. Jody was working neck deep in Ecodiva.

Jody's first big leap forward was when she hired a professional accountant to get her books in order. It helped her regain valuable time and gave her a clear snapshot of the health of her business.

More importantly, it gave her the source of her most and least profitable revenue streams. She discovered that the Kroger account required a large time investment with the smallest financial return. Kroger was selling a large quantity of product but at a wholesale price. Also, for Jody to be successful in Kroger, someone had to demo the product, and she could only be at one place at a time. An investment of time at Kroger meant she had to sacrifice sales somewhere else.

For some, having shelf space in one of the largest grocery chains in the country would be a dream come true. But for Jody, it meant she had to make a choice. She had to answer the fundamental question, what kind of business do I want?

Specifically, should she continue to grow the Kroger account just because it would scale the business when it would bring with it several unfavorable results, including a lower profit margin and the necessity to outsource the mixing and bottling of her product?

We looked at several companies that would take over manufacturing, but each possibility brought more roadblocks and challenges.

In the end, Jody decided to drop the Kroger account. She hired someone to ramp up her social media and started communicating more with her growing list of followers. All of this led to increased sales from her website, and she continued to distribute through local shops and farmers markets.

> *If your business depends on you, you don't own a business—you have a job. And it's the worst job in the world because you are working for a lunatic!*
> —MICHAEL E. GERBER, *The E-Myth Revisited*[3]

Frankly, Jody loves to sell, and she is good at it. It is fun to watch her with a customer as she describes the benefits of her product. She exudes a genuine enthusiasm and believes entirely in what she has created.

Another deciding factor was her health. She needed to take care of herself and get well. The business still required hard work, but it was manageable in the short run. The path she chose gave her more profit, increased sales, and the attention of some potential buyers.

As I am writing these words, Jody just signed her business over to new owners. She couldn't be happier and is ready to start a new adventure.

Many opportunities are lost during negotiations because the entrepreneurs do not know the details of their business.

This is a huge mistake on *Shark Tank* and for your own venture. Being too busy is no excuse when it comes to evaluating your business.

The Sharks have their own reasons for wanting to learn about the current state of your business. Taking this critical step for yourself can make all the difference.

CHAPTER 4

Question One: "Do You Have Any Sales?"

The entrepreneur has finished his or her pitch. He or she has passed out samples, and you know what's next: "Do you have any sales?"

Why is this almost always one of the first questions asked?

Sales cures all!
—MARK CUBAN[1]

Think about it. If you ever ask a business owner, or anyone, for that matter, "How's business?" you want to know if sales are up or down. I recall having conversations with my father-in-law, who owned a hardware business. I would always ask how his business was doing. His reply would be, "We are ahead of last year" or "It has been a bit slow." Once again, sales dollars.

When the Sharks ask about sales, they want to know if you have a viable product. Does the market desire what you are offering? Bottom line—will people take out their wallets and buy your product or service?

Viable is defined by Merriam-Webster as "having a reasonable chance of succeeding."[2]

It's easy for Kevin O'Leary to dismiss a new idea by stating, "Who cares?" or, "You should take it behind the barn and shoot it," but this is the opinion of one Shark. We have seen proof time and time again that one person's opinion—no matter how adamantly expressed—does not determine the viability of a product. History has proven the process of recognizing talent and a great idea can be subjective. Walt Disney was fired and told he lacked imagination. After performing in Nashville, Elvis was told to go back to driving a truck. We could dedicate an entire book to the success stories of people who were told they would never succeed.

In Mr. O'Leary's defense, he takes a logical, no-nonsense approach to business, and in his words, "It's all about the money." If you have been in business a while and do not have sales, you need to ask yourself why. The Sharks would.

How Do I Determine Viability?

When it comes to building a profitable business, choosing a viable product is without a doubt one of the most important pieces of the puzzle. One way to determine viability is to simply fill a need.

The Greek philosopher Plato is credited with the quote, "Necessity is the mother of invention."[3] A need or problem encourages creative efforts to meet the need or solve the problem.

The founder of Simple Sugars, Lani Lazzari, built a successful business while looking for a solution to her own skin issues while she was still in her teens. As a very mature eighteen-year-old, she made what I believe to be one of the most solid presentations in the history of *Shark Tank*. She partnered with Mark Cuban and is now the head of a multi-million-dollar company.

The founder of Drop Stop, Marc Newburger, found inspiration when he dropped his cell phone between the seats of his car, and while trying to retrieve it, his car jumped the curb, nearly struck a pedestrian, and came within inches of hitting a metal pole. He called his friend and inventor Jeffrey Simon to find a way to prevent this from happening and Drop Stop was born.

In spite of the question of sales being the first topic on *Shark Tank*, I am still surprised at the number of presenters who do not see little or no sales as a concern. They are spurred forward by a blind confidence that they have the next best thing because their family and friends told them so. This is *American Idol* syndrome for entrepreneurs. No one wanted to dash their dreams by telling them the truth: "You can't sing!"

> *There are really only two questions to ask when evaluating your business idea: Is there a real need for the product and are enough people willing to pay for it?*
> —BARBARA CORCORAN

I'm not saying that these businesses do not have a chance of succeeding; I'm stating that if you are pitching to a panel of wealthy investors, you must give them a compelling reason to invest besides a hope and a prayer. If you are negotiating with a panel of sharks or laying your business plan out on a card table, you cannot avoid this question. Every entrepreneur who pitches on *Shark Tank* expects it, and so should you.

While gross sales determine viability and your ability to reach a segment of the market, the next question usually involves the history of your company. How long have you been in business, and are your sales increasing or decreasing over time?

The answers to these questions give the Sharks a lot of information. If you have a history of growth over a few years, then one could assume you have a product or service that is attractive to the marketplace and you have the ability to grow a company. On the other hand, a decline or inconsistent sales numbers can indicate the opposite.

As the Sharks' questions peel back the onion, they get a clearer vision of how well a business is really doing. Declining sales may be due to manufacturing issues or a cash flow problem that led to unfilled purchase orders. Inconsistent sales may be attributed to a one-time magazine endorsement or being one of Oprah's favorite things.

Ten seasons of *Shark Tank* have taught us that the Sharks are always looking at the business owner. They observe your decision-making skills, how you handle adversity, and if you possess sales skills. They are looking for character and integrity. They want to know what kind of partner you would be and if you can lead the growth of this business. (More about this topic in chapter 7.)

Bottom line, many deals are made or lost based on what the Sharks learn about the history of your business.

Gross Sales Versus Net Profit

Gross sales volume can be defined as the "grand total of all sale transactions reported in a period, without any deductions included within the figure." *Net* profit represents your business's total profit over a certain period after you total all sources of revenue and deduct all business expenses. You can follow these trends in your business by creating a profit and loss statement (P&L). A P&L is a financial statement that summarizes the revenues, costs, and expenses incurred during a specific period of time, such as monthly, quarterly, and annually.

This is an important distinction and one you must understand to run a profitable business. Gross sales can be impressive at first glance, but when a Shark digs deeper and finds minimal net profit, it can make your business less attractive to an investor and should be of concern to you. Lack of profit in a new business can be caused by many factors, like reinvesting profits to grow the business or investing in a more robust website to handle future growth. These are valid reasons for a weak P&L. However, debt on the company or the inability to produce the product at a reasonable cost erodes your profits. The existence of other equity partners can also divide the profits and make it difficult for a young company to survive.

> *Any business that is not making money after three years is a hobby.*
> —KEVIN O'LEARY.[4]

Being a new start-up is not a deal breaker in the Tank, and many entrepreneurs secure deals while having zero sales. This normally happens on the strength of a unique idea where the Sharks are willing to take a risk or the promise of pending purchase orders, which makes it worth the period of due diligence* to learn more.

Being profitable in your business should be a goal and expected outcome of serving your customers. Rabbi Daniel Lapin, author of *Thou Shalt Prosper*, says each dollar you receive is a little certificate of a job well done or an appreciation of good service. Continuing to invest time and money

---

* Each contestant who strikes a deal in *Shark Tank* must enter a due diligence process to allow the Shark to find out more about the entrepreneur and their business before finalizing the negotiation, Investopedia.com, s.v. "Due Diligence," https://www.investopedia.com/terms/d/duediligence.asp

into a business that is not profitable is an emotional and financial drain. You can avoid this with a solid, strategic plan with clear expectations and timelines. Also, having a trusted advisor or coach can help you gain valuable perspective and objectivity when you get stuck.

Many entrepreneurs have an unrealistic view of their product's potential. That's why sales numbers are so important during the Tank negotiation. The investor wants to know if you have had success with people buying the product or proof of concept. It is more difficult to sell potential and what you believe or hope will happen. Potential sales will not pay the bills or provide you with the capital required to grow your company.

In season seven, Daniel Grossfeld presented a unique twist on hot coffee. His company, Hotshot, gives consumers an alternative to hot coffee on the go from a can. He discovered the concept in Japan, where it was a multibillion-dollar industry, and believed it would be a hit in the United States. After six years of testing and spending over $2 million of his own money and borrowing from his dad and others, he was ready to launch with no idea whether it would catch on in the United States.

I appreciate David's enthusiasm and patience. Hotshot may go on to be a multi-gazillion-dollar company, and I sincerely hope it does. However, I believe he should have explored some other options to test the market. He could have put together a joint venture with a Japanese company and tested their product in the United States. He would have been able to gather valuable market insight at a much lower price point. Instead he spent six years and a lot of money before he had any idea if the product was viable in the US culture.

Set a timeline to make your business profitable, and if it is not making money, you may have to make a hard decision to abort. This is nothing to be ashamed of. Many of us are reluctant to stop investing in a failing venture because of the time and money we've already invested, but we have to know when to quit. Initially you may be discouraged, but your future ventures will benefit from the experience and lesson learned.

What Is the Potential Market Size or Demand?

Market size is defined as a measurement of the total volume or potential buyers of a product or service in a given market. For example, the American Pet Products Association (APPA) states that US pet industry expenditures in 2018 were $72.56 billion.[5] This is a huge market, and I can imagine some of you licking your chops saying, "If I could just get a little bit of that, I would be set!" This is true and I will be the first person cheering you on, but proceed with your eyes wide open. Unless you present on *Shark Tank* or become one of Oprah's favorite things, you have a lot of work ahead of you to carve out a piece of this market.

Gauging market size and demand for your product can be misleading. Mark Cuban considers using the total dollars spent in a particular industry to be a huge mistake in evaluating future results. Just because a particular market is large does not guarantee that your product will be viable. It is easy to think that gaining a small portion of the market could be big for your company, and it can, but you still have to create a product or service that will meet a need, coupled with a sound marketing approach. There are many companies vying for your customers' attention, and you must be prepared.

If there is not an established market for your particular product, this may be a key indicator that the potential is low. Blazing a new trail can be costly and time consuming. There may be a good reason the market is limited.

Considering all the noise in the marketplace, it can be to your advantage to find a *niche* and market to that demographic. Wikipedia defines niche market as "the subset of the market on which a specific product is focused" (e.g., surfers, Harley riders, people who wear bowties).[6]

You must also be clear on what is unique about your product and what sets you apart. Analyze your competition and look for ways you can do it better. Also, examine your product objectively to determine if what you are offering is a trend, fad, or growing market.

Many times you do not need to reinvent the wheel. Improving on an existing idea can set you apart from the crowd. Aaron Krause improved and branded an item that had been around for years and created "America's Favorite Sponge." With the Scrub Daddy's unique feature of becoming firm in cold water and soft in hot water, he and Lori Greiner have become one of *Shark Tank*'s most successful businesses.

One way to determine viability is by creating a prototype and showing it to would-be buyers. A sure sign of a winner is immediate interest and purchase orders. Dan Miller tells the story of a guy who created a new type of weightlifting glove. Instead of getting a supplier to fill his garage with inventory, Dan advised this gentleman to go out and see if anyone was interested. When he received over ten thousand dollars in orders for this new glove, he was ready to set up manufacturing or take the product to an established sporting goods manufacturer and discuss licensing.

I started this chapter with a quote from Mark Cuban, "Sales cures all!" In the video where he said that, Cuban goes on to say, "There's never been a company in the history of companies that's ever succeeded without sales."[7]

"Do you have any sales?" is the first and one of the most important questions you must ask yourself.

Question One: "Do You Have Any Sales?"

Do You Know Your Numbers?

One of the cardinal rules of *Shark Tank* is to know your numbers. We have seen pitches go down in flames because the entrepreneurs were asked questions about the financial details of their business but did not have the answers. You do not have to be a skilled accountant to build a business. You just need to give this part of your business the attention it deserves.

> *For a successful pitch, you've got to know the numbers—or I will eviscerate you.*[8]
> —KEVIN O'LEARY

Tipsy Elves clinched a deal with Robert Herjavec in season five with their ugly Christmas sweaters. When they appeared on the show, they had achieved $800,000 in sales. They now boast gross sales of $100 million. In a season ten update, they shared their struggle the previous holiday season when a loan fell through and they ran up hundreds of thousands of dollars on their credit cards to buy inventory and fill orders. They admittedly learned three things: 1) balance profit and revenue, 2) have a back-up plan, and 3) know your numbers.

When Jody with Ecodiva connected with a competent bookkeeper, she began receiving accurate monthly reports that helped her understand the health of her company and create a realistic game plan to move forward.

As an entrepreneur, there are many tasks demanding your attention. Regardless of its size, ignoring the financial part of your business is a deal breaker and will come back to bite you. Taking a small amount of time to consistently review your financials could make all the difference.

Emily Chase Smith is one of the most talented and smartest people I know. As a former bankruptcy attorney, she knows firsthand why businesses fail. The following is a simple, strategic plan she lays out for you to take care of your money and know your numbers.

20/20/20 Vision

by EMILY CHASE SMITH

I got my first car in 1986. It was a baby blue hand-me-down 1974 Mercedes 240D nicknamed "Bluebird." It's not quite as glamorous as it sounds. The D in 240D stands for diesel. It went zero to sixty in fifteen minutes. It did get killer gas mileage, and among other luxuries, Bluebird sported a double gas tank. However, by the time Bluebird made its way to me, both the gas gauge and the odometer were broken.

Have you ever driven a car with a broken gas gauge and a broken odometer? It's impossible to tell how much gas you have left in the tank. The result is delusions of grandeur that leave you stranded on the side of the road waiting for AAA.

Many entrepreneurs run their businesses as if they have a broken gas gauge and broken odometer—but they don't. The gas gauge and odometer are there for any business owner to see at any time. The gas gauge and odometer will give a business owner knowledge of exactly where they are and where they're going and creates a powerful planning tool. It's not even that hard.

We hear one cry from the Shark time after time: "Know your numbers." Every discussion with the Sharks contains questions about the numbers. Woe be the entrepreneur who doesn't know what it cost to make his product, the cost to acquire a customer, the amount invested in the business, salaries, margin, marketing costs, etc. A wise contestant brushes

Question One: "Do You Have Any Sales?"

up on these numbers before they meet the Sharks. A really smart entrepreneur already knows these numbers. In the same way they can rattle off the name of their business, what they produce, and how they're different in the marketplace, a winning entrepreneur is intimately familiar with their numbers.

It can feel like a long stretch between where you are and that level of knowledge. It can be overwhelming to think of what it would take to move from where you are now to having that amount of recall, but let me ask you this—how much is your mortgage payment? I bet you can tell me. You probably even tell me the cost of your favorite Starbucks beverage with and without an extra shot of espresso. Why? Because those numbers are in front of you all the time. You know those numbers whether you want to or not. This can happen in your business. Before I tell you how, let me tell you a story of two celebs.

In the '80s MC Hammer was a mega star musician, a rapper, and a dancer. He even had his own style of pants. In 1991 Forbes estimated his net worth at $33 million.[9] A mere five years later, he filed bankruptcy listing $13 million in debt. MC popped up again in 2011 owing the IRS over $700,000.[10]

During the same time, Madonna was a young star. Wherever she was performing in the world, she had each day's income and expense faxed to her (this was in the dinosaur days before email). She kept a strong eye on what came in and a tight rein over what went out. Today she's one of the top ten richest recording artists.[11]

What is the difference between MC and Madonna? Both were in the same industry, both were famous worldwide, yet one has continual financial problems and the other is closing in on the Forbes' billionaire list. The key is attention. Madonna paid attention. She knew that no matter how high

33

your earnings, you're not guaranteed financial success. In fact, with higher earnings, you can get in bigger trouble faster.

How can you as a mere nonsinging mortal pay this level attention in your business if you don't hold an MBA in finance? The single best thing you can do is have twenty/twenty/twenty vision. That's not a typo. You want twenty/twenty and one more twenty vision. Twenty/twenty vision in your eyes means that you see the same line of letters at twenty feet that a normal person sees at twenty feet. It's the benchmark of good vision. Twenty/twenty/twenty vision in your business means more. You see the same as a normal person and then some. You know more than the average business owner. You have bionic vision. Here's how it works.

You commit to spending one hour (twenty plus twenty plus twenty equals sixty) each and every month dedicated to the finances of your business. If you're a brand-new business, you want to bump the frequency to every week. If you have a big decision to make or you're thinking about a new expenditure, plan on an hour every week as well. For most businesses generally clicking along, one hour a month is sufficient. It's how you use that hour that is so powerful.

The hour is an appointment in your calendar. It is sacrosanct. In preparation for the hour, you have your bookkeeper gather the most relevant financial documents. For most businesses, that will be last month's profit and loss (P&L) statement. It could also be a P&L comparing last month to the month before or to the same month last year. If this is your first time, keep it simple and use the most recent month. As you engage in this exercise consistently, you will naturally modify the financial statements you use based on what you want to accomplish. Don't get hung up on any of that right now. Just have your bookkeeper pull your most recent P&L.

Question One: "Do You Have Any Sales?"

You're also going to need a timer (could be your phone), a pen, and a piece paper.

Set your timer for twenty minutes. For the first just twenty minutes, all you are going to do is look at your P&L. Take your pen and circle anything that stands out to you. It could stand out because the number is high or because it appears low. It could stand out because you don't know what makes up the number. This first twenty minutes is just for familiarizing yourself with the document in front of you. In this twenty minutes, all you are allowed to do is circle. Don't finish early. Don't take any less than twenty minutes even if you're only looking at one sheet of paper. When the timer dings, you're ready for the next twenty.

Set your timer again, and flip over your P&L so you can't see it anymore. Lean back in your chair, and for the next twenty minutes, allow your mind to tiptoe through the tulips. You don't have a pen in your hand and you're not looking at anything specific. You're just thinking. You are allowing your great brain to make connections between the numbers you just saw on the page and what is actually going on in your business. This is the most powerful twenty minutes you will spend on your business all month long—I promise you. This is where the black-and-white numbers you saw on the page start to connect with the day-to-day operations of your business. This is where you start to think through that payroll number and connect it to the productivity of your staff members and your mind will start to put together a new plan. You will notice where the most income came from on your P&L and start to fashion a way to push forward the pieces of your business that are most effective. You will be amazed at what you will come up with when you spend the full twenty minutes allowing your mind to freewheel.

The timer is going to ding too early, but when it does, set it again for twenty minutes. Flip your P&L back over, grab the fresh sheet of paper, and write like the wind. Everything your great brain discovered in the last twenty minutes is going to hit the paper. The most important will naturally rise to the top. That's why we didn't let you write for twenty minutes. We didn't want to get to the action plan before you had had sufficient time to think it through. The goal is not to end up with a giant list; the goal is to end up with a powerful list. In this last twenty minutes you create an execution plan tied specifically to the numbers of your business. How incredibly powerful.

An hour a month—that's all we ask. No longer are you driving around a 1974 Mercedes 240D with a broken gas gauge and odometer. You know exactly how much gas you have in a tank. You have a plan. Frankly, you also have an incredible advantage to your competition who doesn't spend this one powerful productive hour on a consistent basis. You're ready to win the *Shark Tank*, and even if you don't get to make your pitch there, you end up with all the benefits. A wise Shark knows their numbers, and now you do too.

■ ■ ■

Emily Chase Smith is an accomplished twenty year attorney. She has a strong transactional background reviewing and drafting contracts, business buy/sell agreements, estate planning documents, leases and releases.

Emily served as an Adjunct Professor for Kaplan University, Hope International University, and Anglo-American College in Prague teaching Legal Research, Legal Analysis and Writing, Legal Technology. Legal Terminology, Ethics, Legal and Ethical Issues in Business, Real Property and Introduction to Law.

Emily is the author of *The Financially Savvy Entrepreneur: Navigate the Money Maze of Running a Business* published by Career Press in 2014 and has ghostwritten over 20 books on legal, business, and leadership topics.

Emily lives in Dana Point with her three children, puppy and a garage so full of surf and paddle-boards she has to park outside.

Learn more about Emily at http://emilychasesmith.com/

CHAPTER 5

Question Two: "How Did You Come Up with That Valuation?"

Investopedia defines *valuation* as the analytical process of determining the current (or projected) worth of an asset or a company.[1]

Every pitch must face this question during the negotiation. As viewers, outrageous valuations make for entertaining TV. The moment an entrepreneur states he or she wants a large sum of money for a small amount of equity, we prepare for the fireworks and hope he or she can support the ask.

The Sharks want to buy their equity at the lowest valuation possible while business owners are trying to maximize the worth of their company to give up the lowest percentage possible. This is one of the key components of a lively negotiation. Many times, it comes down to a battle of the Sharks' analytical logic versus the entrepreneurs' passion for their business.

Valuation is an important part of the equation when you are seeking an investment in your business or if you plan to sell it. But if you never plan to sell it, why bother?

Because simply asking, "What is my business worth?" forces you to examine your company in a new light. Approaching your business like you plan to sell it helps you view your long-term goals in the proper perspective for growth. It helps you make better decisions. For example, if you build a business that cannot sustain itself without you, what will happen if you are no longer in the picture?

> *Nothing turns off an investor more than when an entrepreneur comes in with a ridiculous valuation.*[2]
> —KEVIN HARRINGTON

When Jody Norcio with Ecodiva did not plan to sell her business, she was working herself into an early grave trying to do everything. She disregarded some of the key components of running and scaling a business. As soon as she decided she wanted to sell, we uncovered some glaring issues that needed to be addressed. As she began to make changes, she began to enjoy her business again.

Jody eventually sold Ecodiva. However, because she decided to look at the value of her company, it helped her build a stronger, more profitable business.

Passion

The Endowment Effect: The hypothesis that people ascribe more value to things merely because they own them.

Passion is a key ingredient to success. Every entrepreneur who pitches to the Sharks had better have it if they expect to

Question Two: "How Did You Come Up with That Valuation?"

survive in the Tank. But how much is too much? I become concerned when the entrepreneurs are so passionate that they lose perspective of the value of their business and cannot make good decisions or even hear practical advice. You can usually recognize this person by their mantra, "*But this is my baby!*"

Lori Greiner stated in a *Success Magazine* article, "All entrepreneurs think their idea is the best thing ever. They forge ahead and spend a lot time, money and effort on their idea before they've found out if the world is as in love with it as they are."[3]

Is it *really* possible to have too much passion? Barbara Corcoran says yes. This is what she told *Business Insider* about being too passionate:

> Too much passion blinds an entrepreneur, just like a guy who's madly in love. He can't see clearly, he can't listen, and he knows for sure that the girl is 'absolutely perfect!' Being too wrapped up in a love affair with your new business idea doesn't allow you to change what's wrong.[4]

For the last several years, I have been honored to call Dan Miller my friend and mentor. He will tell you that he is an entrepreneur from the top of his head to the bottom of his feet. He has known firsthand the ups and downs of business ownership and openly shares his experience and wisdom to influence and encourage people to find their passion and work they love.

In the following, Dan provides a sobering story on how losing objectivity can lead to personal ruin, along with some guidelines on how you can move forward in your business with a balance of passion and a clear plan.

Avoiding the "My Baby Syndrome"

by DAN MILLER

Jeff was flying high and living large. His engaging personality and amazing sales skills had allowed him to introduce his family to cars, houses, and vacations only dreamed of by most people. And he had just secured total rights to an exciting new medical device invention. This would be his ticket to the ultimate lifestyle. This device solved one of the most pervasive problems in the medical world. The financial margins were staggering as hospitals and clinics were elated to have a workable solution and to eliminate a major liability issue.

But then the challenges began to creep in. There were patent infringement questions, and the FDA was slow in giving necessary approval. But Jeff drew on his trusted relationships to just raise a little money and then everyone would share the windfall. Relatives, church friends, and business acquaintances handed over savings, inherited money, and funds earmarked for retirement, confident that Jeff would reward everyone generously. Uncomfortable questions arose regarding the legality of how money was "invested," "loaned," or "borrowed." The FDA balked at the expected approval for sales in the United States. But Jeff was undeterred. This was his "baby," and he was not known for backing down in the face of difficult circumstances. Weeks turned into months and then months into years. With money being sucked into legal battles, the initial excitement about the device diminished. Friends and family begged Jeff to turn his skills back to his previous areas of excellence—but he knew he could handle just one more obstacle that would clear the path to prosperity and abundance.

Question Two: "How Did You Come Up with That Valuation?"

The drain of hundreds of thousands of dollars reduced Jeff to drawing on more and more of his own resources. The fine family home was sold, the cars were gone, and the vacations stopped. Tensions rose in the damaged business and church relationships—ultimately ending in a painful divorce and alienation of his children. Jeff's tenacity in clinging to his "baby" had destroyed everything of real value in his life.

It takes more than passion and persistence to birth a great business. It takes more than talent and having what appears to be a winning idea. Without a clear revenue stream, the proposed business may be nothing more than a hobby—an exciting use of talent but having few characteristics of an actual business. And there are times when it's best to draw a line, wipe the slate clean, and start in a new direction.

We have to be realistic. Ideas are a dime a dozen. But not every exciting idea can be turned into a great business. Lots of ideas that engage our passions should be kept as meaningful hobbies—additions to a full and exciting life. If you enjoy whittling bird whistles for your grandchildren, go ahead and keep that as a fun activity, with no pressure to make it income producing. Those whistles are very labor intensive and probably have a very limited market. Oh but wait—what about the *Duck Dynasty* gang? Yes, there are exceptions that defy common sense. But trying to duplicate that one example using even altered business principles will likely lead to wasted time and effort. For every success in trying to duplicate the success of the Hula Hoop, Frisbee, Doggles, or Google, there are thousands of failed ventures left lying in the ditch.

As a business coach, I have seen the thrill of victory and the agony of defeat in observing people put legs on their dreams. But here's a suggested guideline for the startup phase.

- In six months, be generating 50 percent of your previous income.
- In twelve months, be generating 100 percent of your previous income.

Few businesses and family relationships can survive the undetermined waiting for an idea that continues to drain finances, time, and energy when months lead into years.

Here's an outline for approaching your idea—no matter where you are currently:

1. *Assess where you are.* Check out similar ideas—what has their history been?
2. *Seek the advice and opinions of competent people.* You'll have plenty who will say it can't be done. Seek out people who are already successful and ask them.
3. *List your best options.* There is never just one option. Should you sell to other businesses or individuals? Should you manufacture locally or overseas?
4. *Narrow it down to three to four approaches.* Don't try to do everything. Be clear and concise. Create a business plan, no matter how simple the idea.
5. *Research and test.* Don't commit thousands of dollars to Google ads. Test small and make adjustments based on immediate results.
6. *Choose the best option and act.* Based on all you know, create a one-year plan and *act*. Commit to one year of focused activity with no hesitation. Dream big, act with abandon, and expect this to be everything you've dreamed of—but then …

Question Two: "How Did You Come Up with That Valuation?"

7. *Evaluate at six and twelve months. Plan for the next thirty-six months.* Are you going to do a full rollout, get additional funding, secure major accounts—or express gratitude for the learning you received and move on to the next idea? Any of those are worthy possibilities.

When I was eighteen years old, having just been accepted at The Ohio State University, I received an $1,800 scholarship. Wow—I already had experience washing neighbors' cars, taking orders for Christmas cards, growing popcorn, and selling excess sweet corn from the family garden. My affinity for seeing opportunity where others saw nothing was already hindering me from having any "normal" view of having money in the bank. I saw that $1,800 as seed money for my next big idea. Yes, I needed it for college tuition, but that tuition wouldn't be due for about six months. In that time I could invest, leverage, earn, recapture my original next egg, and be far better off than my classmates.

I responded to an ad in the back of a magazine like many of you have seen on TV or in a promotional email: "Get into the vending business. You don't have to sell anything. We install the machines—all you have to do is collect the money." Good grief—this was going to be too easy. My $1,800 purchased ten cashew machines that plugged in to keep the cashews warm. What could possibly be more appealing than warm cashews? With the coming cash flow, I envisioned those first ten machines expanding into hundreds carefully placed in ballparks, recreation centers, and family eating establishments. But things didn't turn out exactly as I had planned.

True to their word, the company sent a representative to place the machines for me. His breath should have been my first clue. Unfortunately, that representative had a strong attraction to a particular kind of business and proceeded to position those machines in the sleaziest bars in my hometown. Picture this: a shy, backward, Mennonite farm kid discovering that his new business was centered in places he himself had never been allowed to enter.

Guess what else didn't turn out as I expected? Do you know what happens to cashews under heat if they are not stirred about every four hours? They mold! I immediately began to get calls from these sordid establishments telling me to get those machines out or suffer the wrath of their inebriated customers. I picked up my ten precious machines and hid them in an old chicken shed where, to his dying day, my dad never knew about this particular story of my stupidity. When it came time to pay my tuition, I had to get out and hustle to recapture that lost money. I squeezed in odd jobs around my already busy schedule of farm chores and college classes. A couple of years later, I sold those vending machines for essentially scrap metal—selling the whole lot for three hundred bucks. It was my first of many painful but instructive lessons that looking for a quick buck is typically a recipe for disaster.

The key to real success is not about jumping on the latest, greatest idea you read about in a magazine or some website. It's about knowing yourself so completely that you can identify work you will find meaningful, fulfilling, and profitable. Work that blends your passion and talent and leads to generating significant income.

You think I hate the vending business, vowing to never again get suckered in? No, I love vending businesses, and I continued to look for better opportunities that still allowed for the passive and recurring income experienced in few other

Question Two: "How Did You Come Up with That Valuation?"

businesses. Years after that initial fiasco, I purchased my own drink vending machines and placed them in a fitness center I owned. They were a very profitable addition to the revenue stream in that business. Today I am an author, speaker, and coach. One of the resources we offer is a personality profile to help people know how their behavior aligns with particular career choices. That personality profile happens to be our hottest-selling product—outselling even my *New York Times* bestselling books we also have available.

Let's think about how that profile is delivered. People put in their payment information at any time day or night, get a unique access code, complete the questionnaire, and receive their thirty-five-page report immediately. I never see or talk to them. Does that sound vaguely like a vending machine? Of course it is. I essentially have an electronic vending machine. But I have advantages that a cashew machine could never offer. Instead of loading up a truck and driving across town, I can reload my "vending machine" with a click of the computer. Instead of being limited to my own hometown, I can provide my product to customers anywhere in the world. I love my vending business.

Don't be afraid of failing. We learn from our mistakes and failures. Those are not designed to stop us but rather to educate us for future success. They are a necessary part of moving to higher levels of success. If you are always successful, it's unlikely you've really stretched yourself to see what you're capable of doing. Like a high jumper, if you always clear the bar, you don't really know how good you could be. It's only when you trip the bar that you have a true indication of where your limits are. It's in "failing" that we grow and expand our possibilities.

But as Kenny Rogers reminded us years ago,

> You've got to know when to hold 'em
> Know when to fold 'em
> Know when to walk away
> Know when to run.

Yes, I believe in burning the boats. I believe in persistence and following your passion. As a career coach I've told thousands of people to "do what you love and the money will follow." But without guidelines and clearly defined strategies, those broad philosophies can lead to business and personal disaster. There is a time to walk away from your idea.

If you're not making money after six months of focused efforts, check to make sure this is a real business.

Your business idea is not "your baby." It's an idea, a concept, or a possibility that can be nurtured to exhilarating prosperity—*or* it can be killed and buried with your head held high and your integrity intact as you move on to future successes.

You don't make those choices with a baby.

■ ■ ■

Dan Miller, President of 48 Days LLC, specializes in creative thinking for increased personal and business success. He believes that meaningful work blends our natural skills and abilities, our unique personality traits and our dreams and passions. Dan is active in helping individuals redirect careers, evaluate new income sources, and achieve balanced living. He believes that a clear sense of direction can help us become all that God designed us to be.

Dan is the author of the widely acclaimed *48 Days To The Work You Love* and *No More Mondays*. He has been a guest on CBS 'The Early Show,' MSNBC's 'Hardball with Chris

Question Two: "How Did You Come Up with That Valuation?"

Mathews,' and *Fox Business News with Dave Ramsey Show*. He hosts a weekly podcast that is consistently ranked #1 under careers on iTunes.

Learn more about Dan at https://www.48days.com/

■ ■ ■

How Do I Determine the Value of My Business?

We have concluded that knowing what your business is worth is important, but how *do* you determine an accurate valuation?

First, let's look at your business from a Shark's perspective. As an optimistic entrepreneur, we know you are passionate and believe everything will turn out exactly as you envisioned. The Sharks, on the other hand, know from experience that a lot of things can go wrong. They want a substantial return on their investment to compensate for the risk they are taking.

Mark Cuban admitted to *Success Magazine*, "Valuation is not a simple formula. In spite of what the business might be worth, you'll see us negotiate because we need to get enough equity to repay us for our time, and that allows us to share in the upside."[5]

Each presenter always starts their presentation with the desired investment and the percentage they are willing to give up. You can quickly calculate what they believe the business is worth. For example, if an entrepreneur asks $50,000 for a 10 percent equity in their company, you know they are valuing their company at $500,000 ($50k/10% = $500k).

The Sharks may counter with an offer that is 50 percent of the entrepreneur's valuation or $50,000 for 20 percent based on our example above. They are not guessing and pulling numbers out of the air. They are using proven methods to calculate what the business is expected to achieve in years to come.

49

During the negotiation, the Sharks ask questions about sales, inventory, and cost of goods while evaluating the entrepreneur's ability to grow the company and be a good partner. This is all in an effort to determine if they can get their money back plus a nice return on their investment.

Future earnings are only part of the value of a business. The Sharks have an affinity with certain products or types of businesses based on their own expertise and experience. If they cannot get excited about your product or bring value to growth, they will usually go out. However, there are exceptions. If a business is a sure thing, the Sharks will fight for a piece of it because all roads lead back to making a profit.

There are many methodologies when valuing a business. One way is to calculate a multiple of earnings. This involves multiplying a company's profits by a certain value. You may hear Kevin O'Leary ask, "How much profit did you make last year?" Usually, the follow-up question is, "How much did you pay yourself?" This gets them close to a net profit. If the entrepreneur values the business at $3 million with a net profit of $100,000 last year, he or she is asking the Shark to pay a multiple of thirty times profits. At this point the Sharks may not believe the business is worth that. General thinking on *Shark Tank* and elsewhere is to use a multiple of eight to ten times profits for this type of valuation.

Depending on the size and type of business you have, there are many ways a business can be evaluated. Valuing the hard assets of a business, such as inventory, machinery, and real estate, is one method and is fairly straightforward. It becomes more difficult when you have a service business with few, if any, hard assets. At this point, you have to lean more on earnings, sales history, and customer acquisition costs.

Valuation is a big part of *Shark Tank* negotiations, and you should become familiar with the process. There are a

Question Two: "How Did You Come Up with That Valuation?"

number of books and online resources available to help you understand and see what method works for your business. My advice would be to get the help of a competent professional to help you valuate your business.

CHAPTER 6

Question Three: "How Did You Finance Your Business?"

This question always comes in two parts, "How much money did you have to start your business?" and, "Where did you get the money?"

The answers give the Sharks clues into the business's financial state. If you personally financed the start of your business and currently have no debt, it can make your business more attractive for an investment. If your company is carrying a large amount of debt or you have sold off a portion of your equity to raise capital, it can dilute your value and be harder for a Shark to see a way to invest.

Like it or not, it also gives the Sharks a view of your decision-making and money-management skills. They need to be able to trust you with their investment and know you are capable of managing the growth.

Personally, nothing frustrates me more than seeing an entrepreneur invest large sums of money, regardless of its origin, into an idea that is untested. This is very dangerous and can be discouraging when you find out that there is little demand for your product. It also places an unnecessary strain on yourself and your family. When you become overly financially invested, it becomes hard to turn back. It may provide some well-needed drive to execute your business plan and sell your product so you can recoup your money, but you may lose objectivity in the process.

Some businesses do not require any money to get off the ground. I started a directional sign business several years ago out of the back of my truck that still generates a five-figure income today. Other start-ups require cash to get started, and some cost more than others.

Many of the entrepreneurs on *Shark Tank* are skilled at raising capital. However, having a lot of capital can be dangerous for a young business. Unless they are disciplined, they tend to overspend and create an artificial marketing environment that cannot be sustained over time. You can hear the air being sucked out of the *Shark Tank* when presenters reveal that they have invested hundreds of thousands of dollars of their own money and borrowed from friends and family with little to show for it. They may be taking way too much time to launch or the product may not be viable. At this time you may hear someone say, "Take it behind the barn and shoot it!"

However, the Sharks get excited when they hear a successful pitch for a debt-free business that has been bootstrapped for a few hundred dollars and has generated thousands of dollars in sales.

Daymond John, who started FUBU with $40 worth of hats and turned them into $6 billion in sales, said this about money in his book *Power of Broke*:

> I believe very strongly in the Power of Broke. This is simply the concept that when you are broke, you have no other choice but to find a way around

Question Three: "How Did You Finance Your Business?"

the money issue. You don't have the funds to just go out there and do what you want. You are desperate in a way, and this leads to: Creativity, Innovation and Thinking Outside the Box.[1]

According to an article in *Small Business Trends*, a third of small businesses get started with less than $5,000 and 58 percent got started with less than $25,000. Other studies have shown that 26 percent of small businesses can be started with zero capital.[2]

- Hewlett Packard was started with $538.
- Dell Computers was started with $1,000.
- Spanx was started with $5,000.
- Barbara Corcoran took a $1,000 loan and turned it into a real estate empire

Many *Shark Tank* entrepreneurs use crowdfunding as a way to test interest in their product while raising needed capital for their venture. Crowdfunding by definition is *the practice of funding a project or venture by raising many small amounts of money from a large number of people, typically via the Internet.*[3] Kickstarter and Indiegogo are two of the largest crowdfunding platforms, but there are many to choose from.

Even Kevin Harrington, inventor of the infomercial and Shark on the first two seasons of *Shark Tank*, is in the crowdfunding space. He has joined the team at Digitz to create the crowdfunding initiative InventureX.

It can be disheartening when you dream of starting your own business and believe it requires a large amount of capital that you do not have. If you have very little money or you are not an expert in raising capital, my hope is twofold: 1) that you will understand that you do not need a lot of money to get started and 2) to spend what you have wisely since most businesses fail because they run out of cash.

Kent Julian is a man who knows how to develop a plan and get it done. He has proven that bootstrapping your way to success is not a dream—it's a reality. As a matter of fact, one of his goals as an entrepreneur is to help people move from *dream* to *do* in what matters most.

You are really going to enjoy the following section where Kent defines bootstrapping, along with three strategies for how to apply it to your own business.

"Bootstrapping"

by KENT JULIAN

I'm privileged to deliver the keynote speech at association conferences, business meetings, and to young entrepreneurs in student organizations such as DECA, FBLA, BPA, and more. The number-one question I'm asked when speaking, both onstage and off, is how to start a business. Even more, people want to hear the details behind how I started a successful and profitable lifestyle business.

The word that best describes how I started Live It Forward, LLC is "bootstrapping." What follows is a brief definition of bootstrapping, along with three key bootstrapping strategies for how to start your own business.

Bootstrapping Defined

Bootstrapping is defined by Entrepreneur.com as "*financing your company's startup and growth with the assistance of or input from others."* It also refers to *"stretching resources—both financial and otherwise—as far as you can."* The major benefit to bootstrapping your business is *"it is one of most effective and inexpensive ways to ensure a business' positive cash flow. Bootstrapping means less money has to be borrowed and interest costs are reduced."*

For me, bootstrapping was the only option I considered when starting Live It Forward, LLC. Kathy and I had been married fourteen years and had been debt-free except for our house the entire time even though I was a youth pastor, which is not a very lucrative line of work, and she had been a stay-at-home mom before our children started school. In other words, we knew how to stretch a dollar and didn't want to go into debt to start a side business. I was willing to hustle like crazy and invest every ounce of sweat equity I had because I strongly believe in the big is little and little is big principle.

Three Keys to Bootstrapping Your Lifestyle Business

There are many things to keep in mind when bootstrapping your business, but here are three key strategies that were enormously important for me.

1. Investment and Business Mindset

Embracing the proper mindset is critically important when launching your business since you will be investing long hours at the beginning with little financial return for your efforts. This is why I embraced my bootstrapping adventure with an *investment and business mindset.* Let me explain.

First I decided to view the bootstrapping journey ahead as an *investment* with no downsides. You see, in the beginning, I asked a lot of "what if" questions. What if I can't gain any traction? What if I make major mistakes? What if all my side hustle doesn't produce results and it takes ten years to get this business off the ground? As you can see, "what if" thinking can paralyze you!

To overcome "what if" thinking, you have to change your mindset, and that's exactly what I did! Instead of viewing the entrepreneurial journey as a problem to be solved, I started seeing it as an opportunity to invest in. I figured as long as I didn't bet the farm and do something like take out a second mortgage to start my side business, there was no downside. I would meet people I'd never meet if I didn't take this entrepreneurial journey. I'd likely learn things I'd never learn otherwise. Plus, new opportunities were bound to open up to me that would have never opened up before.

Did you catch the message? There are no downsides to the entrepreneurial journey ahead of you, so don't get paralyzed by "what if" thinking. Even if you don't get your business off the ground, the benefits of just traveling the path are enormous and will likely open up opportunities that are unimaginable to you at this moment.

This proved true for me. Within the first three years of bootstrapping my business, I learned more about starting a business than I could have learned in a decade of just reading books or listening to podcasts. I was also blessed to become great friends and business affiliates with Dan Miller, *New York Times* best-selling author of *48 Days to the Work You Love*. Additionally, one of the books I published was highlighted at the Mega Book Marketing Conference, which allowed me to share the stage and be interviewed by Mark Victor Hansen, coauthor of the *Chicken Soup for the Soul* book series.[4] Finally, one of the largest church-ministry publishing and training companies in the world, with whom I trained and that I wrote for during my bootstrapping years, asked if I was interested in

Question Three: "How Did You Finance Your Business?"

a new position overseeing their youth ministry department. I wasn't interested because of my commitment to my business, but the fact that they asked me is a testimony of how new opportunities open up when you pursue your business dream. Again, there are no downsides to pursuing the bootstrapping adventure ahead of you, so don't get stuck asking yourself "what if" questions. This journey ahead of you is not a problem to solve; it's an opportunity to invest in!

With that said, if you want to succeed as an entrepreneur, you must also embrace the second word in the *investment-and-business* mindset and treat your bootstrapping journey like a *business*. This means a lot of things, but at the core it means you have stop dreaming about what could be and start hustling big-time. Even more, you have to create structure in your routine that allows you to hustle and take action.

For me, even though I was the executive director of a national youth organization that served approximately two thousand groups in all fifty states and was traveling one hundred nights a year when I started bootstrapping, and even though Kathy and I had three children in elementary school, I carved out a minimum of fifteen to twenty hours a week to work on my lifestyle business. It definitely wasn't easy, but it was doable. What I discovered is I had to scale back from all the fluff in my life so I could scale up my business. No more mindless TV. No more time-consuming activities that didn't add significant value to my life. I even scaled back from volunteering, at least for this season of my life. My life basically revolved around four things: 1) spending time with Kathy and our children; 2) working my full-time job; 3) working on launching my lifestyle business; and 4) investing in personal development through journaling, goal setting, reading, and exercising (especially running). That's all I did for three years, yet during these years, I became a better husband, father, and person because I forced myself to scale life down to only those things that mattered most.

Practically, here's the power behind scaling down your life so you can scale up to at least fifteen hours a week for bootstrapping your business. If you work fifteen hours a week on your side business and do this for forty-eight weeks (take one week off each quarter to rest and recover), that's seven hundred twenty hours a year, which equals eighteen forty-hour workweeks in one year. This means during a three-year period, you will work the equivalent of an entire year of forty-hour workweeks. If you really hustle and work smart, that's plenty of time to get your side business off the ground!

Note: It took me three years of working fifteen to twenty hours each week to launch Live It Forward to the point where I could quit my full-time job.

2. Fifty-Fifty Money Management

A powerful strategy behind bootstrapping your side business is you don't have to pay yourself a salary if you have another job. That's why I encourage all my lifestyle business coaching clients to resist paying themselves from their side-hustle business for as long as possible to invest their profits into the **fifty-fifty money management** strategy described below.

Personally, I invested the *first 50 percent* of Live It Forward's profits into a cash fund. This one action helped me build a strong enough cash reserve that I was able to leave my full-time job before completely replacing the salary from that full-time job. When I did quit my full-time job, I calculated that if Live It Forward only produced the same amount of revenue it had during my last year of bootstrapping, I could provide for my family for two years on the salary I could pay myself along with the cash-reserve cushion I had built. This gave Kathy and me tremendous peace when I quit my full-time job because we knew once I could give full-time attention to my lifestyle business, it would likely grow substantially, and that's exactly what happened!

So, what did I do with the other *50 percent* of the profits from my business? I invested it back into the company. I purchased equipment, built a website, and marketed my services and products. But even more, I invested in the most important asset of any lifestyle business. I invested in myself! I attended conferences, hired coaches, and more. I saved both time and money by learning from people who were already doing what I wanted to do!

The first year in business Live It Forward's total revenue was only $4,000. The second year it was $24,000. The third year it was $68,000. Again, during these first three years of bootstrapping, I never took a salary. This means by the time I committed to Live It Forward full-time, I had a cash reserve of $48,000. Additionally, I had invested $48,000 back into the business, with most of that money being invested into learning everything I could about building and growing a lifestyle business and how to be a motivational speaker who actually gets paid to speak. In my first year of working Live It Forward full-time, revenues almost doubled to $128,000.

3. Stick-to-it-tiveness

Just know, your greatest competitive advantage in starting and growing a lifestyle business is stick-to-it-tiveness. By no means am I the smartest or most talented person in any room, but I do stick with it! What I've discovered about stick-to-it-liveness is if you are persistent and learn all you can from each step you take, you will outlast 90 percent of your competition. This automatically puts you in the top 10 percent. I don't know about you, but I love those numbers!

■ ■ ■

Kent Julian is a professional speaker, dual business owner, committed family man, fish-taco lover, and proud bald guy. His goal is to help you and your team move from DREAM to DO in what matters most. Kent was the executive director of a national organization with over 2,000 affiliates after which he pivoted to start two business — one personal brand business and most recently a real estate business. Now he primarily spends his time keynote speaking, consulting, and hosting the Live It Forward Show (a podcast dedicated to helping people move from DREAM to DO both personally and professionally). You can also find Kent enjoying a run, pursuing the perfect fish taco, or hanging out with his wife and kids.

Learn more about Kent at https://liveitforward.com/

■ ■ ■

Captain Happy

John is one of the most optimistic and yes, happy people I know. He embraces the title of Captain Happy that was bestowed on him by a satisfied client. You would like John. When you first meet him, you could assume that he hasn't a care in the world. He will immediately tell you how blessed he is, but like most success stories, he's known his share of obstacles.

John is candid that his business has never been about making money. He contributes his success to fear of failure that started from an inability to read well. His pride would not allow him to ask for help and let people know he had dyslexia. He would read ahead of the rest of the class and memorize passages to be ready if the teacher called on him. He states, "I just worked harder than everyone else."

Question Three: "How Did You Finance Your Business?"

John is not alone is this regard. He joins a long list of people who suffered from dyslexia and went on to become very successful. That list includes Sir Richard Branson, Albert Einstein, and Steven Spielberg, to name a few. We can't leave out the Sharks, Barbara Corcoran, Daymond John, and Kevin O'Leary, who are also dyslexic. They all consider the learning disability not a disability at all, but an advantage.

After being terminated from his mid-level management position, John spent two depressing weeks worrying about how he would provide for his family. A local businessman told John, "If you are not too good to push a mop, I will pay you to clean my convenience stores." He jumped at the opportunity, and his cleaning company was born.

He started with a $5,000 loan from a relative that he has since paid back. After fifteen years, his company is generating sales in the seven figures, and it employs over a hundred people.

Just when he thought he had it all going his way, he was diagnosed with stage 4 cancer. In the blink of an eye, he was faced with a whole new set of challenges. Even though this diagnosis and the intense treatment stretched him and his family to their limit, he continued to be optimistic and fight.

Today, John has a new perspective and intends to make the most of what he has been through. He is more excited than ever to grow his company and is currently dealing with the challenges of clients wanting his services in other parts of the country.

I have no doubt that John will tackle this challenge just like all the others and make the best decision for himself, his family, his employees, and most importantly, his customers.

CHAPTER 7

Question Four: "Do You Want or Need a Partner?"

When the Sharks ask entrepreneurs about their background, they have a clear motive, and it can mean the difference between a deal or no deal.

Each may be looking for different characteristics, but they all want to know what kind of partner you would be. Are you resilient? Are you decisive? What is your skillset? Many times the answers to these questions trump the viability of your business if they believe you have what they are looking for in a partner.

Barbara Corcoran stated on her Instagram feed August 2019 that she looks for three characteristics in an entrepreneur:

1. A great salesperson: If they can't sell me during their pitch, how are they going to build a business?
2. A clear communicator: Are they clear in their answers, and do I get what they are saying?

3. A competitive drive: Live and breathe competition, and when the chips are down, have the drive to compete, rise up, and keep going!

Lori Greiner believes in being clear and concise as well. She told *Business Insider* that you need to be able to describe your business or product within two sentences.[1] She also told *Success Magazine* that character and integrity were high on her list when looking for the right person to partner with.

Jack and Carol MacDowall determined that partnering with a Shark for their business, Moosehead Kettle Corn, did not fit their business plan. For various reasons, other entrepreneurs need a skilled partner to help them take their business to the next level.

This is a big decision to consider and a two-sided coin. First you must decide if you want or need a partner, and second, you must determine if you would make a good partner. For that reason, Deb Ingino has come to our rescue!

Deb is a dear friend and has joined me regularly on my *Shark Tank Fan Podcast* to bring her wisdom to our listeners. She has many years of experience navigating corporate America and mentoring leaders while developing strategic partnerships that has elevated her company, Strength Leader Development, to one of the premier coaching businesses in the country.

How to Create a Great Strategic Partnership

by DEB INGINO

The right partnership can take your business to levels well beyond its current scope. Conversely, a wrong partnership can ruin your business, relationships, and reputation. Choosing the right partner to share the equity in your business is absolutely critical to your success.

When it comes to partnerships, you need a good defense—a solid legal agreement. And perhaps more importantly, you need a good offense—a solid partnership that will work together and stand the test of time.

Every attorney will tell you, "Consult with your attorney before entering a partnership." And that is wise advice. But I will tell you that even the most masterfully crafted legal agreement will not prevent an absolute failure on either side of the partnership if the partnership is simply a bad match. Consult with an attorney, but remember that a legal agreement is not going to save a partnership, and it is not going to prevent you from getting into a bad partnership. What it will do is help you get out of a bad one.

Where Partnerships Fail

Undefined Relationships: A partnership is not a sibling relationship. Partners are not blood brothers, twins, or BFFs. On the other hand, partnerships don't have to be cold, clinical connections, either. Partnerships are respectful business relationships.

Uncommitted Partners: Partnerships begin as fine silver. But over time, the relationship can begin to tarnish. Once the honeymoon stage is over and the partners begin to lose the awe they once had for each other, they can begin to lose respect for one another. One partner may start pulling back and not contributing as much as they did at the onset. The other partner may sense the inequity. Things begin to cool in the partner relationship.

Unclear Boundaries: Another issue I have seen is conflict of interest. I have seen individuals come into a partnership where they happen to have a technical skill—let's say programming—and while they are the president of one company, they are doing programming on the side for other industries. I have to tell you, if you are running a business, moonlighting on the side until your business has taken off in a dramatic fashion without it detracting from your current work is tough to pull off. If doing this affects your commitment to the partnership in any way, it is a big no-no. I have even seen partners moonlighting in one business on another similar business. That is unethical.

On the other hand, I have seen individuals who have equity and partnerships in multiple businesses who successfully contribute value to each business. These are those who are approaching partnership in a very serious way. Their commitment and contributions to each are steady, and additional partnerships in no way detract from those currently in place. They realize it is not the time they spend on the business that matters but the contribution they make in the business. This is the more strategic, ethical, and beneficial approach.

Unplanned Strategy: Early in your business, you may need a cowboy or cowgirl—someone who can take the reins and wrangle through the ideas and details to get things rolling. As the business progresses, you need more of a tour guide—someone who is a stable navigator, who can look off into the horizon and envision new ideas for growth, and who is constantly aware of changes in the trail that might affect your business. Where many businesses go wrong is in not understanding that these two distinct roles usually are not found in the same person.

Unharnessed Ego: Another area where partnerships go wrong is failing to harness ego power in the right direction. Anyone in an equity position in a business obviously has to have some degree of ego about them because they want to accomplish something and make a contribution. But when that ego deviates from focus on creating a more effective strategy, executing a better plan, or increasing contacts to focus on self, it can very quickly kill a partnership. A strong ego can feed a business, or in its demand to be fed, starve it.

These are the pitfalls of a partnership and the reason attorneys include an exit clause in every partnership agreement. Legal agreements are for protection, and they make a good defense. But the main focus of this section is to help you create a good offense—to help you determine how not to end up in a bad partnership to begin with.

Where Partnerships Flourish

A successful partnership is a unique coming together of two or more highly capable individuals with a few things in common. *Shark Tank* is a great example of how two or more highly capable individuals with a few common characteristics can create a very successful business enterprise.

Reasons for Creating a Great Partnership

Capital: Often, when you think of bringing in an equity partner, you think about capital. Capital (meaning funding) is certainly one piece of the equation, but it is only one piece. It may help smooth some of the bumps in the road, but it can just as easily mask some of the bigger underlying problems. Capital is no substitute for a good plan and a good business model.

In capital considerations, these questions must be addressed and agreed upon in writing. How much is needed? How much will each party bring to the table financially? Is it equal capital for equal ownership? What is the intended use?

Contacts: There are various types of contacts: strategic contacts, strategic alliances, potential joint venture partners, advocates, and allies.

If your business involves a product that can be sold in big-box stores, then obviously a great strategic partner for you would be someone who has a network of contacts in big-box stores—someone who has already broken into the market and has a great relationship with them. Keep in mind that just because someone has sold to a big-box store doesn't necessarily mean they have a great relationship. They may just be another vendor in a very large pool of vendors. The key is to find someone who has the ear of the decision maker, the buyer, or the CFO or CEO. Those are the people you would want to consider for a partnership. If you are bringing on a partner to create strategic connections, be sure he or she has the right connections. Tying compensation to desired results will provide a measure of protection as well.

Strategy: Sometimes you need a thinking partner. This is more than just an advisor, mentor, or coach. It is someone who will actively and regularly strategize with you in the business and who has a great track record of success. Not only are they thinking with you, but they also have skin in the game.

I read an interesting story about Warren Buffett. I learned that he actually has a partner that few know exist. His name is Charlie Munger. Interestingly, Warren and Charlie grew up

Question Four: "Do You Want or Need a Partner?"

a few miles from each other but only became acquainted later in life. They currently live in different states. They do not work together on a daily basis. But they are strategic thinking partners. Though you see Warren Buffett as the face of Berkshire Hathaway, there are actually two very intellectual, business-savvy minds behind it, each very serious about the business's success and very respectful of the other's ideas.

If you are going to think with someone to this level, you must be assured that your focus aligns. One way to test the waters is to bring them on as a consultant first. Have them work with you on a project. Date before you marry into a committed partnership. This will help you determine if they are consistently focused on solid strategy or simply a one-trick pony with a few good ideas and nothing more. Observe how they do their research, how they think, and their values. You are looking for someone who will be with you as Charlie Munger has been with Warren Buffett—committed for the long haul and consistently strategizing to improve and grow the business. Do the work of vetting whether or not a potential equity partner is a good fit for you strategically.

Strengths: Each person is uniquely gifted and wired with certain strengths, gifts, and talents. There are things you can do well that others cannot do well, and frankly, there are areas where their strengths exceed yours. This complement of strengths is essential to a business. Though our inclination may be to hire and work with people just like us because we relate to them, we must actively look for people who are not like us. If you hire someone who looks, acts, thinks, and does just like you do, why do you need them…and why do they need you?

To partner up, look at their strengths and be clear that you are not looking for them to merely put in time but for them to contribute their strengths in a measurable way that delivers results. Tying the financial reward directly to results is an excellent model.

Finally, a word about the spotlight: decide up front who takes the lead. Oftentimes that is dictated by percentage of equity, but frankly, that is not always the smartest approach. Deciding who should be the public person or if both can be is important. Most successful strategic partnerships have one leader who is more comfortable being out front, and that level of communication is in their strengths zone.

Winning Matches for a Great Partnership

Values Match: How do you find a strategic partner who is a good match for you and your business? You must start with values, because if your values don't match, little else matters. You must trust that they are a person of integrity, and you must share a common work ethic. You won't find this on a legal document, and they don't teach it in business school, but in my experience, it has been a critical factor. When values are aligned, it creates a core from which individuals with different experience, strengths, and perspectives can work and serve together.

Vision Match: I recently heard a story about a partnership that is unraveling because the one partner who started the company with his vision is working with a partner who no longer buys into that vision. He wants to change the vision, and the founding partner says, "No go. This is my vision. This is my baby. This is what I am driving toward."

Just as you can't go into a marriage expecting to change your spouse, you can't go into a partnership expecting to change your partner. If a partner is looking to change the vision, you have the wrong partner. The common vision is the basis of a successful relationship, and it must be there from the start. In fact, a common vision is a good indicator that you have the right partner. You need a partner who sees what you see and is excited to work alongside you to bring the vision to reality. You will have differences of opinion on how to accomplish the vision and different perspectives, and that is good. But the vision must remain firm. It is foundational.

Goal Match: With matching values and vision, the stage is set to create goals for what you want to accomplish together. There is a great example in Hollywood. Ron Howard, who most of us might know from *The Andy Griffith Show*, is now a director. Brian Grazer is a producer. A lot of people would call them the Hollywood odd couple. This unlikely duo has gone on to create movies together like *Frost Dixon*, *The Da Vinci Code*, *Angels and Demons*, and many, many more. I read somewhere that Ron Howard said, "Our lives are so different, and that is one of the interesting things about our partnership. It is built upon this shared sense of what we want to accomplish together and what we have in common."

Characteristics of a Great Partnership

Mutual Respect and Awe: Partners must have enormous mutual respect for each other and the strengths and gifts that each brings to the table. There will naturally be some waning of appreciation for talents over time, but there needs to be enough of an awe factor that the residual level of respect is still very high. Otherwise, your partnership will fall into the diminished respect, diminished contributions cycle.

If you are giving away your equity begrudgingly, then you don't really believe in that person enough. You really don't. When you find the right partner, you will give away whatever percentage of equity makes sense to get those talents in your business for them to partner up with you.

Egos and Spotlights: As we saw in the story of Warren Buffett and Charlie Munger, there has to be a way to decide who is in the spotlight and who is not and how to navigate the partner egos. How do you allow each other to bring the fullness of your respective egos in the right direction without having it become a liability in the wrong direction?

I'll give you an example. I've seen a partnership where one partner was exceptional with sales, marketing, branding, and strategy; and the other partner was exceptional with technology. In technology-related discussions, the technology partner was the one who got to make the final decision because that was his swim lane. In discussions about strategy, branding, sales, or marketing, the other partner was the designated decision maker. That is one easy way to match egos and spotlights.

Another easy way to match them is to decide in advance who will be the one overall leader. And no matter what, that person is the decision maker. Now in the case of Warren Buffett and Charlie Munger, it is Warren Buffett. But he respects Charlie's opinion so much that he has actually allowed it to sway his own decision in many cases, and he said he has been very glad in those cases when he did.

Two as One: The most important thing for a winning match is that you want two individuals working as one. A great example of a working partnership is Bill and Melinda Gates. I have seen many family businesses absolutely crumble—both the family and the business—because they didn't get a lot of things right. They didn't have values or visions that matched. Just because your family owns a bakery doesn't necessarily mean you want to be or should be a baker. The mutual respect and awe sometimes is not there in families. Sibling rivalry kicks in. Egos and spotlights can be a real issue. Battles for attention are common. There can be mortal wounds in a family and business relationship. In a family, it

Question Four: "Do You Want or Need a Partner?"

can be very difficult for two individuals to work as one. It really does require mutual respect and absolute awe of each other and the focus on sharing what you want to accomplish together. And that is why I think Bill and Melinda Gates do this so successfully. They have tremendous respect for each other. Intellectually, they respect each other's strengths. They have learned together. They have served together. And in the end, their relationship trumps the business. So at the end of the day, they don't consider themselves to be a success if the business or foundation is successful but their family is not. They have been very careful to make sure their relationship stays intact, that their marriage and parental commitments do not suffer on the altar of a working partnership.

A Culture Match: You need to make sure your partner is also a match for your team and the team culture. They must have a heart for your people and a leadership style that is complementary to yours. While your approaches may differ slightly, you must present a united leadership front to the team.

Storms and Successes: As business partners, you are going to hit pockets of turbulence. That is a given. You want to make sure that, as you're hitting those bumps, your partnership is secure. Always remember to attack the issues and not each other.

Just as much as you will weather the storms together, you should celebrate the successful reaching of milestones as well.

I'll never forget hearing a CEO talk about his first overseas trip to France with his business partner. They were looking at manufacturing facilities for a product they were developing. They arrived early in Paris, and after a great dinner, they went out for a walk. Two young businessmen in their late twenties, they found themselves laughing in disbelief that they were actually there.

As they passed by a cool sort of uber-chic men's store, this partner spotted a leather jacket that made him stop in his tracks. He exclaimed, "Oh, man, look at that jacket! Holy cow, I have never seen anything like that in the US. When I make it big, that's the jacket I know I'm going to want to wear."

Unbeknownst to him, his generous and kind-hearted partner took note and purchased the jacket. In time, as success came, he presented the jacket to his partner in celebration of their success.

At their core, business partnerships are relationships. You must choose your partners wisely, stay committed to the vision, labor together through the storms, and celebrate the successes.

■ ■ ■

Deb Ingino, CEO of Strength Leader Development. A highly sought-after executive mentor, consultant and speaker worldwide, Deb is well versed in business operations and in the importance of asking key questions most business leaders won't ask themselves. She brings deep experience in leadership development, strategy, high performance team building, global operations, and management, design, product development and training to her work. Her passion is for leading people to discover and maximize their strengths as well as those of fellow team members, while offering advanced strategies to achieve high performance.

Learn more about Deb at https://www.strengthleader.com/

CHAPTER 8

Question Five: "Do You Have a Patent?"

Q & A

with AARON KRAUSE
Inventor of Scrub Daddy®
and Successful *Shark Tank* Entrepreneur

In season four, Aaron Krause walked into *Shark Tank* asking for one hundred thousand dollars in exchange for 10 percent equity in his business, Scrub Daddy, a versatile cleaning tool with a smiley face design that will adjust its scrubbing texture with your water temperature. After some intense negotiation, he secured a deal with QVC Queen Lori Greiner for $200,000 for 20 percent equity. That was October of 2012, and Krause has never looked back. He has gone on to be the most successful business ever to appear in the Tank, building profitable relationships with leading retailers such as QVC,

Bed, Bath & Beyond, Walmart, Home Depot, and Kroger, to name a few.

I have enjoyed multiple conversations with this dynamic inventor and entrepreneur. In this interview, we discuss how he got on this path to discover his passion and his thoughts on patents and trademarks.

Q: What was your first invention, and how old were you?

A: It's interesting that you would ask me that because I happen to remember exactly when that was. I was about ten years old lying in bed. My dad liked to keep the thermostat down low, so it was cold in the house but warm under the sheets. When I finished reading my book, I didn't want to get out of bed to go turn the lights off (this was way before they had the Clapper). The next day I went to my dad's tool shed and found these old wheel casters, and I mounted them together using nails and dental floss, the longest "rope" I had, and made a pulley system between my bed and the light switch so I could turn my light on and off while lying in bed. My next invention involved rewiring the phone system in my parents' home because they told me I couldn't have a phone in my room. I got caught with that about a year later when my parents called the phone company to complain about static in the line.

Q: Do you believe people are born creative and curious, or is it something you can develop?

A: I have several knee-jerk reactions to this question. My first reaction is, of course you are born with it. You are either creative or you are not. You are either an inventor or you are not. You are either an entrepreneur or you are not. I think that is true in some respects, but other thoughts ring true. All people have creative ideas. What makes the difference, what makes you an inventor or entrepreneur, is whether you act on your ideas or how quickly. I have had so many people tell me these great ideas that they just never acted on. So, I think all people are creative, but most people are just not motivated enough to act on their ideas. Probably only one out of a thousand people act, and out of the those, most will get discouraged with the process and quit.

Q: *Is there any advice you give budding inventors about what they should* not *do?*

A: First, do not go around telling all your friends and family about your inventions. Keep it to yourself while you hire a *patent* attorney, not a regular attorney. You need one well versed in patents, trademarks, copyrights, and intellectual property. I found out the hard way the value of an attorney by trying to submit a product for patent myself. I got a letter back from the patent office that I could not even understand. If you have a true invention, start with these three steps.

1. Do your own research. Go to uspto.gov and research your idea. You may find out that someone else has already invented your product.
2. Call a patent attorney. They will do further research and give you an educated opinion on whether they think your patent will be approved or not.
3. Apply for a patent. Market and sell while your patent is pending. Do not wait until the patent is approved because you need to create revenue and establish your product in the market to be able to afford to protect your patent. Patent pending puts you first in line for the patent. Then you can talk about it, go to market, and become the name brand.

Q: Why shouldn't you talk to people? Shouldn't you find out if there is a market for your product before you spend all that money on development or attorneys?

A: Because people talk. You may run across an unscrupulous person who will steal your idea. Almost every product I have has been knocked off. Because I patented my idea and was first to market, I had the money to fight the lawsuit and win. If you don't patent your idea right away, your attorney can give you a nondisclosure form for people to sign before you talk to them that will give you at least some protection.

One more thing—there are invention companies that promise to help you patent and develop your product and get it to market. In my opinion, you should *never* use one of these companies. They basically take the money you could have paid your attorney to protect your idea. They own your idea, and they can do whatever they want with it at that point. It's a roll-the-dice move of people who have an idea that they are probably not ever going to do anything with anyway. They're just giving it away, and if something happens, great. I have had people want to partner with me but can't because their product is owned by one of the companies. If you want to do this and never plan to do the work yourself, go ahead, but I would not recommend it.

Q: Is a patent the only way?

A: No, sometimes a patent is the absolute wrong way. When you have intellectual property, knowledge, a process, or an ingredient, the last thing you want to do is apply for a patent. The reason is you have to disclose everything about how you make it, what it is made of, and all its attributes, and that is now available for everyone to see. They can change one small thing about it and get around your patent. For example,

Question Five: "Do You Have a Patent?"

Coca Cola is never going to patent their product. Basically, do I want to tell the world how I do this, and can they use that information against me?

Q: How much does a patent cost?

A: Depending on the type of patent, it can cost seven to eight hundred dollars to get started. I have received a patent in a year for a thousand dollars. A patent can cost up to seven or eight thousand dollars if it gets rejected and you have to start over. It could take up to five years or longer, and the cost goes up the longer it takes.

Q: What are the different types of patents?

A: I am really only familiar with the two that I have gotten: design and utility. A design patent is the ornamental shape or design of the way something looks. It has no function; it is just the way it looks. It is a simple patent and very limited scope. For example, I have a design patent on the smiley face on my Scrub Daddy sponge. The material is it made of is intellectual property, and I do not want a patent on that because then the formula would be out there for everyone to steal. A utility patent is much more expensive than a design patent, usually three to seven thousand dollars. A utility patent protects the article's function.

The www.USPTO.gov site describes a design and utility patent as follows:

> *Design Patent: Issued for a new, original, and ornamental design embodied in or applied to an article or manufacture.*
>
> *Utility Patent: Issued for the invention of a new and useful process, machine, manufacture, or composition of matter or a new and useful improvement thereof.*

Q: Talk to us about trademarks.

A: I have applied for five trademarks and have sold some of them. Trademarks and patents are actual tangible assets, things of value that you can actually sell, a huge difference between patents and trademarks. Patent is on the product or process. The trademark is how you phrase something or the design of a logo…something very specific about the shape that represents you, your product, or your company. Trademarks do not expire while patents do expire. Can you imagine if Coca Cola could lose their trademark and someone else could assert they are *The Real Thing*? That's an important distinction.

Q: How do brands play a part in trademarks?

A: The Scrub Daddy logo is trademarked. We felt it was important for our brand that when you see the words *Scrub Daddy* and the design, the way it is laid out in the shape with the smiley face on a sponge, that's mine. I own it and someone else can't use it.

Q: How did you come up with your valuation? What would you tell someone going into Shark Tank *about their valuation?*

A: I hope you did your homework and know your valuation, because so many people go on *Shark Tank* and don't. The correct way is there is no correct way. It basically comes down to what a business is worth and whatever someone would pay you for it. How good are you at convincing someone of the value of your company? You better have the evidence to back up why you think your company is worth X amount. Tell them the sales, your patents, intellectual property, and exclusive deals. Tell them your long-term plan and your history. Sell yourself, and sell your product. Be confident. Be realistic.

Question Five: "Do You Have a Patent?"

You have to understand you are pitching to multimillionaires and billionaires who are investing their own money, not a venture capitalist or some bank. You also have to consider what they bring to the table in expertise and success. Don't insult the Sharks by overvaluing your business and undervaluing what they bring to the table. If you do, the Sharks will be out and you will not even get the chance to pitch your product.

Q: If you could go back and speak to your ten-year-old self, what would you tell him?

A: Most of the things I would tell myself would be about girls and not about patents. LOL. I really believe this journey has led me to exactly where I am. Would I really want to go back and change any of it? No, it's all those experiences that got me here today. You really need to have some hard knocks in business, just not the major ones that knock you out.

Q: Final thoughts?

A: I would like to finish with America and our comeback in the business and economic world. Creating businesses, even if you have to import some things, is so important and means so much to our country and our local economies. This country was built on entrepreneurs and inventors. We need creative thinkers. We are good at coming up with new ideas and concepts and turning them into businesses, not just copying someone else's idea. Business is coming back to America in a huge way, and if you have the spirit of an entrepreneur, an idea or invention is so much bigger than yourself and just the product. Look at what you're doing for your community and your country. I think it's beautiful.

■ ■ ■

Aaron Krause is an accomplished entrepreneur and inventor with more than 25 years of experience in patenting and manufacturing innovative products. With products in major big-box retailers and acquisitions by such industry giants as 3M Company (NYSE: MMM), Krause is a self-made entrepreneurial success story who prides himself on hard work, dedication and imagination.

Krause received national attention when he appeared on the hit ABC show *Shark Tank* with his invention the smiley face Scrub Daddy scrubber sponge. After successfully pitching the sharks Krause received a capital infusion from prolific inventor and celebrity mogul Lori Greiner. Since then, Krause and Greiner have sold tens of millions of "the smiling sponges" to well-known retailers including QVC, Bed Bath & Beyond, Wal-Mart, Target, Kroger, Home Depot, Lowe's, Ace Hardware, Giant, Walgreen's, and Amazon.

As a result of continued media, marketing, and business development efforts, Scrub Daddy has exceeded $150 million in retail sales since the *Shark Tank* appearance and continues to gain recognition as a household brand. The product line, which was developed with extensions and iterations, was also spotlighted in The Wall Street Journal as a contender in the half-billion-dollar sponge market.

In 2014, Scrub Daddy was named the "Most Successful Product" in *Shark Tank*'s history and continues to hold that prestigious title. In 2016, Krause won Ernst & Young's Entrepreneur of the Year Award for Greater Philadelphia, and Scrub Daddy won Philadelphia Business Journal's Best Places to Work 2016.

Learn more about Aaron and Scrub Daddy at https://scrubdaddy.com/.

CHAPTER 9

Question Six: "Is Your Product or Company a Brand?"

Brand? I'd Like One of Those, Please!

by JIMI GIBSON

You've heard the term *brand* many times. Is it your business card? It's your logo, right?

Could you stand on a street corner and explain or demonstrate your brand to passersby? Better yet, how do your customers or prospects perceive your brand?

What does a brand mean for your business? Why should you care?

If you complete the exercises in this chapter, I will guarantee you that you'll have spent more time than the majority of business owners crafting the most valuable asset on your balance sheet—your brand.

Before we get too far, let's start with a little history lesson.

85

The word *brandr* is a Norse word meaning, "To burn." Products and livestock were burned with the producer or owner's mark. The term is probably most recognized by the practice of burning the rancher's mark on cattle—a brand. Before traditional fencing was used, a brand was the only way the owner of cattle could tell them from all the others grazing in the fields.

During the industrial revolution in the United States, new products were being created, and manufacturers needed a wider market. New distribution channels opened because of an expanding railroad system that provided access to these new markets. However, the mass-produced products had to overcome the trust of locally produced goods. Packaged merchandise was labeled to increase the familiarity of the benefits and features of unfamiliar goods. Early brands such as Campbell soup, Coca-Cola, Juicy Fruit gum, Aunt Jemima, and Quaker Oats began to grow and spread across the United States.

Around 1900, advertising agencies began to spring up and use a new form of trademark advertising. The slogans, jingles, and mascots that some brands have maintained even today were born. Around the 1940s, manufacturers became increasingly aware of the relationships consumers were establishing with the products they consumed. The practice of purposely crafting a personality for products to present to a specific type of customer introduced the practice of branding.

How do you build your brand? Please understand, before you start any branding or marketing approach, you'll need a strategy and a plan that reinforces everything else you're doing.

If you complete the exercises in this chapter, you'll have some major skills in your repertoire:

Question Six: "Is Your Product or Company a Brand?"

- You'll be in alignment with why your company exists.
- You'll be crystal clear on how you will be seen by your target market.
- You'll know how to communicate with your best clients.
- And most importantly, you'll be doing all of this from the core of why you are uniquely you.

I prefer using a notepad for the first draft of each exercise. Personally, I think more clearly with the ability to scratch through lines, doodle, and insert arrows and edits freely. You might prefer your favorite note-taking software. Whatever method you choose, dedicate some time in a place where you won't get distracted.

Don't try to accomplish all the exercises in one sitting. Your brain needs time to work things out over the course of a few days or weeks.

Exercise 1

I want you to take inventory of everything you're doing right now that has visibility to your customers or potential customers. You're going to make a big list. Think thirty or forty entries, not five.

I really mean everything. Leave nothing out. I want you to list websites, brochures, business cards, voicemail messages, pens with your logo, intake forms, envelopes, and invoices. When you think you're done, dig deeper. Walk yourself through your product or service delivery from the perspective of a client and write it all down. Do you have a phone script in your head that you usually go over with a potential client? That's an item. What happens after they visit your website? Do you provide anything after the sale? Would you ever mail (email or snail mail) your customer or prospect? Do you have a few social networking components? Write it all down. Have one line for each visibility item. If your customer or prospect can touch it, hear it, see it, or experience it, write it down.

Now that you have the master list, I want you to go through each item, one at a time. Beside each entry, write down the feeling, impression, or nugget of information a client or potential client receives from this interaction. Don't generalize. Be as specific as possible. Consider the *emotion* they feel. If I go to your website and everything is the color red—the logo, the menu bar, and headlines—clients may immediately say to themselves, "Wow, this person sure likes red." It's that basic. If your business card has a logo with a flower on it, your client may be asking, "What does a flower have to do with this business?" Look at each item from the perspective of someone who knows nothing about you or your business.

Are you a consultant? Your intake form may be printed on nice paper in multiple ink colors. The information is clear and well written. The reaction from the client may leave the impression, "Nice. This person has their act together. Okay, I'm supposed to fill out this form and return it within three days. Got it."

I know that sounds like a weird assignment, but it's vital to where we are going. We just need to get a baseline of the current situation.

If you are just starting your business and you don't have anything to write, here's what I want you to do. What are your knee-jerk reactions about what you are thinking about producing? What's on your top-ten list? Are you thinking of a website? Brochure? Logo? Maybe you only have five things.

Question Six: "Is Your Product or Company a Brand?"

Now, next to each one of those, write down what you want to communicate to a client through that piece. I don't want long descriptions. A few words are more than enough. Think emotions and benefits. How are they supposed to feel after visiting your website or receiving your business card? Got it? Write it down.

That's it. Don't rush through the process. Spend some time. Immerse yourself. Be true to what you want to accomplish, and be honest in your answers.

Sometimes we can't see the forest for the trees. When you created one of the items on your visibility list, you may have thought you were communicating one message while you are actually communicating something else entirely. Maybe you didn't put much thought into the item the first time. There's always time for a do-over. Find a friend or relative who has the patience to give you honest feedback. Explain why this exercise is important to you and what you are trying to accomplish. Consider organizing a small focus group of friends who know you well and others who don't. Take notes. Don't get offended. (Hint: Free food and drink creates a friendly environment for genuine feedback.)

Did you complete exercise 1? What was the point?

Well, here's the big secret. Your brand is simply the sum of all experiences your customer has with you. It allows them to form an opinion about you based on the benefits you provide them at a pure *emotional* level.

Your brand is your website, plus your business card, plus your phone voice, plus the invoice you send them at the end of a project. It's not a series of isolated activities but a complete ecosystem that combines to produce a value proposition, competitive advantage, and loyal following.

Branding as a verb is really a false way to think about it. Consider it a noun that you will protect at all costs. We want to build a brand, not perform branding. If you grasp this simple concept, you just got your postgraduate degree in the reality of the brand.

You are not done with exercise 1 yet. Go back through your list. If the intended impression the customer is receiving from the interaction is not what you want, write down the intended impression you desire. You'll have to reverse engineer the approach to get the result you want.

This is tough. You'll need to step back and put yourself in the mind of your potential customer.

If you objectively looked at the paper you are using for your business card and the impression was, "Cheap paper. I hope they don't skimp on their service with me." Guess what? You'll need to reprint your business cards on different paper if you want to get a different reaction.

Hold off on revamping every item on your list. The "What Now" section of this chapter will reveal the secret to editing your visibility list the right way.

Exercise 2

Now I want you to describe what you do, how you do it, who you do it for, and what value you bring.

This is your core reason or purpose for being in business. It's the one thing that will never change about who you are and why you do what you do. Some refer to this as your mission statement. I like to say core purpose. The visual of a rock solid core is important for the long haul of your company. Crafting one is a little tricky, but it is vital to the rest of your brand. Your purpose statement should be broad enough to carry you through but pinpoint the emotional reason you exist. Make sure you refer to the four points: what, how, whom, and what value you bring.

Question Six: "Is Your Product or Company a Brand?"

Here are some examples to get you started.

> *Skype's mission is to be the fabric of real-time communication on the web.*
>
> *It is the mission of Advance Auto Parts to provide personal vehicle owners and enthusiasts with the vehicle-related products and knowledge that fulfill their wants and needs at the right price. Our friendly, knowledgeable, and professional staff will help inspire, educate, and problem-solve for our customers.*

How invested are you in the words? Did you just write a bunch of fluff to fill the space? Take some time and think through a statement that will endure the test of time. Filter your mission down to the core components that will guide your product offering and service model.

Would it make sense for Advance Auto Parts to sell airplane parts? Not now because a personal vehicle won't fly you to work. However, their mission is crafted to allow for the possibilities of the future. Their free battery installation is simply an expression of their mission to, "Inspire, educate, and problem-solve."

Exercise 3

We've had exercises on how your customer views the interaction with you. You've crafted a core purpose.

It's tough to avoid the fluff and be as specific as possible. I hope you're proud of yourself. You should be. This is the type of thing that Fortune 500 companies do. They hold fancy corporate retreats at expensive resorts and have sub-committees that report back to a core group. Lots of late nights are spent putting dreaded PowerPoint presentations together to present to their peers. Decisions like this can take months or years to refine, rewrite, and communicate to all employees. And you did it by yourself!

Why did I put you through this agony? We're treating this like a business, not a hobby. Small Business Trends suggests that 44 percent of startup businesses do not survive past four years.[1] Why is that? I'm no research expert, but I believe entrepreneurs jump into a business, get all their "stuff" printed, get a website programmed, and slap their logo on some ballpoint pens. But they fail to do the work up front that leverages their uniqueness and passion in a way that will make them profitable and sustain them through the tough times. When you don't operate from a strong core, then you can be consumed with chasing carrots. Chase too many carrots and your business doesn't resemble the company that started a few years prior.

Ready to craft a few inspiring core values?

The values of your company will allow you to stand firm and deliver the mission. Your business or brand is visible to your customer. Remember lesson 1? You create a business card, and there is some reaction in the mind of a customer or potential customer.

There are four layers that flow from your core values to the impression on the customer or potential customer. In other words, your core values ground your business. From those core values flow the beliefs, thoughts, and eventual actions your company expresses to the world. Remember the list of visibility items in exercise 1? Layer 1 represents every item on that list. (See below.) Each of those items should have originated from a core value from layer 4. Keep reading.

Let's walk through each layer.

Question Six: "Is Your Product or Company a Brand?"

Layer 1—the Outside

The impression is everything you say or do, a client can see or hear. It's how you say it and how you do it. It could be your website, your logo, or your phone voice. Got it?

Layer 2—What You're Thinking

What your customer sees or hears comes from what you, as the business owner, think about—your mental talk. Ideas swirling around in your head can affect what you do and how you do it, what you say and how you say it. You thought it would be a good idea to put a certain photo on the card, so you did it.

Layer 3—What You Care About

What you think about comes from your attitudes and opinions. What are you passionate about? What do you hate? What do you love? What must you involve yourself in? What will you stay away from? These attitudes and opinions affect what you think about, which in turn affects what you say and what you do.

Am I going too fast?

You had an opinion about what photo should go on the business card. You thought it would be a good idea to print it that way. You did. The customer saw the card.

Layer 4—What Do You Believe In?

Your attitudes and opinions come from your core values. What core values will you stand for? Did they come from how you were raised? Did something happen in your life to shift your values? Did you start this business because of a strong belief you have? Usually an organization will have three main core values.

Advance Auto Parts has three core values: inspire, serve, and grow.

Usually, the company will have a short paragraph to further explain what these values mean. You will probably have personal core values that you'll transfer to the organization, as they are appropriate to your product, service, or industry. If you're honestly a funny person, humor may be a core value you'd transfer from your own personality to the business. This value would influence the actual text on a website or be the tone of personal interactions. Warning: Tasteful humor can be an asset in a stuffy business category. Off-putting humor can be the recipe for disaster.

So, to review, your core values are at the center. They affect your attitudes and opinions, which affect your self-talk. Your self-talk is expressed in what you say and what you do and how you say it and how you do it.

Each layer affects the other layers. The outside layer, layer 1, is easiest to change. It's simple to change what you do and say, but it won't affect the core values without tremendous leverage and repetition. The inner core is hardest to change—layer 4. However, if you make a conscious decision to change a core value, based on a shift in your business strategy or life experience, the other layers change immediately.

Diets don't work because you are simply changing layer 1—what you eat. To get lasting results, you've got to change your core belief about eating and nutrition. Your attitudes and opinions will change. What you think about will follow, resulting in a behavior change about what you consume.

Beware of value words that have been used over and over. *Honesty, integrity,* and *quality* are good words. However, any successful business should operate from these core values. Dig deeper. What makes your business unique? An accounting firm with a core value of *creativity* may get some strange looks

Question Six: "Is Your Product or Company a Brand?"

unless it is backed up by a value-based rationale. Explaining that you are committed to "creative accounting" could turn a perceived negative into a memorable differentiator.

Exercise 4

One of the biggest pain points I hear from my clients is, "I need more customers." When I throw the follow up question back, "Okay, who's your best customer?" I often get a blank stare.

You first have to know *who* is your best client before you can go out and look for them. Have you really thought deeply about who you want to do business with? I know that sounds like a backward question. Many business owners truly think, *Hey man, I'll do business with anyone. If they're payin', I'm playin'.* Unfortunately, that's the way most businesses get sidetracked, lose focus, and eventually end up hating their work. Your passion turns into a job when you're doing things you don't want to be doing for people you don't want to be doing them for. You become trapped in a business that is controlled by your worst possible customer. If you are an introvert, can you work with extroverts? Do you like working late at night but seem to attract customers who only want morning appointments?

If you've been in business a while, you know what I'm talking about. If you're just starting your business, be forewarned. Don't shackle yourself. Create a business that inspires you to find the best clients who truly appreciate the gifts you provide through your products and services.

Here's my advice for making it through this lesson. Your company needs a personality. I heard a wise person once say, "If everyone likes you, you don't have a personality." There's some truth to that saying. If you're trying to be all things to all people, what do you believe in? Don't worry about those who don't get you. There are plenty who will if you truly know yourself and express it freely. You will have those clients for life. Customers like this wouldn't think about going to someone else because they believe in your company, and they connect with you in a way that they just don't feel with your competition. That's the true essence and value of a brand. It's loyalty. It makes them wear a T-shirt with your logo on it.

Right now, you are going to write a biography of your target market. I want to know where they live geographically and a detailed description of their home. I want to know if they're male or female. How old they are? (Hint: thirty-five to fifty is not an age. Pick the exact age.) What they do in their spare time? What makes them angry, happy, or sad? How much money do they make? What do they do with that money? Do they have children? What do they drive? Are they frugal? Do they recycle? How do they dress? If you could take that person out to lunch, what would you talk about? What restaurant would you go to? What are their television and internet habits? Do they read? Books or magazines? Name the titles. What's their favorite movie? Pizza topping? Please get as detailed as possible. You should know this person inside and out.

You may have different services or products that have different types of customers. Pick your top income-producing one. If you don't know your ideal customer right now, pick the one that you want to be the top income producer. This is the one you'll use for the exercise.

Craft a nice paragraph that gives you a sense of who this person is, what they're all about. You can even name them if you like. Ad agencies entertain themselves by picking names like Adventurous Andy or Serious Sally. It sets the tone for the personality slant that predisposes them to do business with you. Think of your target market as a living, breathing caricature of all the best demographics and personality types that will make you overjoyed to have them as a client.

Give your paragraph to your focus group. (Remember exercise 1?) Have them name friends and relatives who meet this description. You may have just identified some potential customers for life.

What Now?

Hopefully you've completed some of the exercises and will work hard to finish them all. While this chapter is a small chunk of my complete branding series, you should have a clearer sense of what growing a brand involves.

Do you now see the danger in printing a business card or launching a website without thinking this through? You want each impression to build on all the other touch points to the brand.

It's not necessary to display your mission statement on your website or marketing materials, but every business decision should be held up against this filter. If what you're about to do doesn't fit, don't do it. By the very nature of adhering to this corporate compass, your customers will infer what the company is about and trust will grow as you fulfill the promise of your core purpose.

In each interaction you have with your customer (layer 1 of exercise 3), be sure at least one of your core values (layer 4 of exercise 3) is identified as the originating source of the interaction. So if one of your core values is *fun*, then your marketing pieces, customer service approach, or product packaging could express your attitudes, perspective, and design of what you think is fun.

The more you know about your ideal customer, the more authentically you can speak with them. Use their language.

Let them know you are aware of their cares and concerns in how you craft your communication. Your goal is to create the impression in your customer's mind, "Hey, they know me."

Live the principles in each of the exercises. Bring them together for a unified approach to the way your company operates, the products you produce or services you provide, how you communicate with your ideal prospects, and how you retain your best customers.

Dig deep and put the work in up front. Your efforts will be rewarded with a steady flow of customers you call friends.

■ ■ ■

Jimi Gibson, known as "The Branding Magician," is a speaker, entertainer and branding expert. As a keynote speaker, sleight of hand artist and creative director, Jimi speaks to corporations about the role of creativity in business. The secret to developing creativity skills can be learned. These "tricks" can impact the bottom line of an organization in "amazing" ways. He has performed across the U.S. and Canada including the MGM Grand in Las Vegas. He is currently finishing his first book.

You can learn more about Jimi and Branding at http://jimigibson.com/

CHAPTER 10

Question Seven: "What Is Your Plan?"

Shark Tank negotiations and business plans both want to know:

- Where are you today?
- Where are you headed?
- How do you plan to get there?

Questions about sales, valuation, personal background, and inspiration for your idea are all part of question one. The answers provide the Sharks a great deal of information to determine if you are worth the risk of an investment and if you would make a good partner. For various reasons, many never make it through this stage and leave without an investment. Those who survive phase one and want to build a successful business should prepare for questions two and three, "Where are you headed?" and "How do you plan to get there"

Where Are You Headed?

In this phase, the Sharks' personal biases take center stage. Mark Cuban may believe that taking your product to retail is a terrible idea and you should grow online, while Lori Greiner believes Bed Bath and Beyond and QVC will make you a millionaire! Of course, we can't forget Mr. Wonderful and his creative licensing deals.

> *An idiot with a plan can beat a genius without a plan.*[1]
> —WARREN BUFFETT

The motive of each Shark is to determine how you plan to *scale your business* (i.e., to grow and expand in a proportional and profitable way). You may recall Mark Cuban lacking interest in a business that cannot scale up to $50 million or more. From their standpoint, they are looking for a return on investment that can only be accomplished by the business growing exponentially.

There are multiple paths to market and grow your business, but you must choose wisely. Each distribution channel requires different levels of infrastructure and personnel, along with their own set of challenges.

Distribution channel is defined by BusinessDictionary.com as "the path through which goods or services travel from the vendor to the consumer."[2] Simply, how will you get your product or service in the hands of your customer?

A century ago, options were limited for business owners. Customers were limited to trading or purchasing from local merchants or businesses. The biggest limitation was geography. In the twenty-first century, entrepreneurs have multiple avenues at their disposal to distribute their goods. You have to decide what option best fits your business model and type of product.

Choosing a distribution channel can be a complicated issue if you allow it. In the beginning, you have to ask, "Who is my ideal customer, and what is the best path to reach him or her?"

Most entrepreneurs start out with a *direct to consumer* model that can require nothing more than a website. This is the easiest entry point because anyone can create an online presence from a card table in a spare bedroom. Just like it states, this model eliminates the middle man and is a direct path to sell your product or service to your customers. Other direct models include having a retail store, assembling your own sales team, and phone sales.

Direct distribution can be the most profitable and allow the owner to have a better connection with their customers but it can more difficult to manage on a large scale.

Indirect distribution, also to referred to as wholesale distribution, relies on third parties to perform most distribution functions. This model can be much simpler for the owner to manage and the best path to scale growth because it frees them up to concentrate on the core aspects of their business. The most challenging part is that you have to trust the third party with manufacturing and customer interaction while adding layers of cost, vendors, and bureaucracy.

Franchising

Another way to expand without owning each location is *franchising*. When you have developed a successful model, you can duplicate it by granting another party the right to use your tradename, systems, and processes that you have proven. This is another means to scale your business and can help you duplicate your efforts without needing the up-front cash to open multiple locations yourself.

Licensing

Mr. Wonderful is usually the first Shark to tempt an entrepreneur into a licensing agreement. In most cases, the entrepreneur has created a product in a very competitive industry where it will be difficult to gain market share. It some cases it would make more sense to partner with an existing company in your industry than try to reinvent the wheel.

Licensing is a business arrangement in which one company gives another company permission to manufacture its product for a specified payment. Licensing your patents, designs, and intellectual property can be one of fastest ways to grow your business and be more profitable.

It can go both ways. You may have an idea similar to BedJet but it may be difficult to break into the mattress industry. However, one of the existing manufacturers may want to license your idea and incorporate it into their existing offering. As sales are generated, you will receive a royalty or commission. The profit may be less than if you sold the product directly, but your overhead and responsibility are greatly reduced.

You may want to enter into a licensing agreement with a company to use their intellectual property. If you have a product that will sell to a specific demographic, such as college sports, you need permission to use the name of the sports team and their logo on your product. You will have to pay royalties for the privilege. Having access to that demographic can bring credibility to your product and boost sales.

When determining the best distribution model to serve your customer, the questions and answers will change as your business grows. What it needs in the early stages may be different when your business reaches new levels of growth. Daymond John started FUBU by selling his products in front

Question Seven: "What Is Your Plan?"

of the New York Coliseum, and his distribution network has grown exponentially over the years.

You may recall back in chapter 1, Moosehead Kettle Corn chose consistency over scale. The challenges of going big were not worth the potential benefits. They chose to continue serving their customers in a way they enjoyed and at a size they felt comfortable controlling.

Sarah Nuse, co-owner of Tippi Toes Dance, appeared in season two of *Shark Tank*. During our interview, she explained how turning down a deal with Mark Cuban was the right decision. Cuban wanted to grow at a rate of fifty franchises per year. That type of growth would have demanded so much of her time that it would have prevented her from being the wife and mom she wanted to be. After ten years, they have thirty franchises and are looking to expand internationally. Sarah and her sister, Megan Reilly, are profitable and happy and built their business on their own terms.

Every situation is different. There is not a one-size-fits-all plan for any business, especially in today's marketplace. You must make plans and decisions that are right for you. The proper direction for you may be entirely inappropriate for another.

For example, two gentlemen went through a financial setback where they were forced to file bankruptcy. During their struggle to come back after this setback, they met and became close friends. Both of them took their passion and created very successful businesses that are thriving and growing today. They have both written bestselling books and serve a large audience with their experience and teachings. What sets these two entrepreneurs apart is the path they chose to build their business.

One is in the final stages of building a large office building that houses his business and a team of hundreds of employees.

He has a thriving business model that has been voted best place to work in his region. His business approach matches his personality and is required to support the many facets of his enterprise, including a radio show, online presence, book sales, and training seminars that he conducts around the world.

On the other hand, the other gentleman bought a home and some land with an old barn on the backside of his property. He renovated the barn, creating a private office with an apartment, warehouse, and area that will seat about fifty people. He enjoys the solitude of his morning walk to his office and the peaceful surroundings to write and be creative. He also boasts about the fact that he has no employees and uses contract labor to complete all of the needs of his business.

Both men have created very successful businesses and enjoy an affluent lifestyle, but they have two entirely different approaches that suit their personalities and ways of life. Keep in mind, these two entrepreneurs chose their path, it was not an accident.

You can create the life and business you desire if you have a clear vision of who you are and what you want. As this example demonstrates, an entrepreneur's personal and business goals are intertwined and must be considered in the decision-making process.

What Is Your Plan to Get There? Creating a Strategic Plan

You can count on Robert Herjavec to be one of the first people to ask, "What is your plan?" By this time, he has heard where you came from and where you are now. Now he is ready to hear your vision and plan for the future. This is a

Question Seven: "What Is Your Plan?"

pivotal moment in the *Shark Tank*. All of the Sharks are listening, and they may or may not agree on your chosen path for your business.

Creating a written plan clarifies the specific action steps that will be taken to achieve your vision. It provides clear direction and prevents you from drifting. It also provides an organized document that you can take to a banker, investor, or buyer to get funding. Out of the dozens of advantages a business plan creates, maybe the greatest is to keep you focused on the most important aspects of your future growth. As I mentioned earlier, it is easy to get bogged down in the everyday details a business requires. Reviewing your plan regularly will help you become a better leader and manager and stay focused.

> *Our goals can only be reached through the vehicle of a plan, in which we must fervently believe, and upon which we must vigorously act. There is no other route to success.*[3]
> —PABLO PICASSO

A couple of years ago, I listened as Dave Ramsey interviewed Dan Cathy, president and COO of Chick-fil-a, on his *Entreleadership* podcast. I was intrigued by this interview because Mr. Cathy was discussing his vision for the company by the year 2020. Chick-fil-a started in 1946 and in 2014 boasted sales of over $6 billion, with nineteen hundred locations in the United States. They have had forty-seven years of positive sales growth, and after the interview, I understood why.

Mr. Cathy went on to explain how they were currently studying companies that were already at the volume and size he envisioned for Chick-fil-a in 2020. They were implementing the infrastructure to prepare for the growth well in advance. This type of vision and planning helps a company avoid many of the pitfalls that can occur if there is no plan at all.

We have watched as *Shark Tank* entrepreneurs explain their setbacks, and for some it has been detrimental to their ability to secure a deal. It was not the setback that hurt them but the entrepreneurs' lack of resilience and an adequate plan to overcome that setback. The Sharks understand that obstacles will occur from running a business. They want to know if you are the kind of person who can deal with adversity and keep moving forward.

It is impossible to predict all of the pitfalls and setbacks that can occur in a business, but you can minimize the obstacles through a strategic plan. One valuable tool for evaluating yourself and each aspect of your business is the SWOT analysis.

SWOT Analysis

Albert Humphrey is credited with inventing the SWOT analysis in the 1960s to help Fortune 500 companies produce long-term planning that was executable and reasonable. I was introduced to this valuable tool during a business-planning workshop conducted by entrepreneur and CEO Chuck Bowen.

SWOT analysis is a business tool designed to evaluate a subject's strengths, weaknesses, opportunities, and threats. It is laid out in a simple quadrant format that allows you to pinpoint internal and external factors in your business. Strengths and weaknesses are internal while opportunities and threats are external.

Question Seven: "What Is Your Plan?"

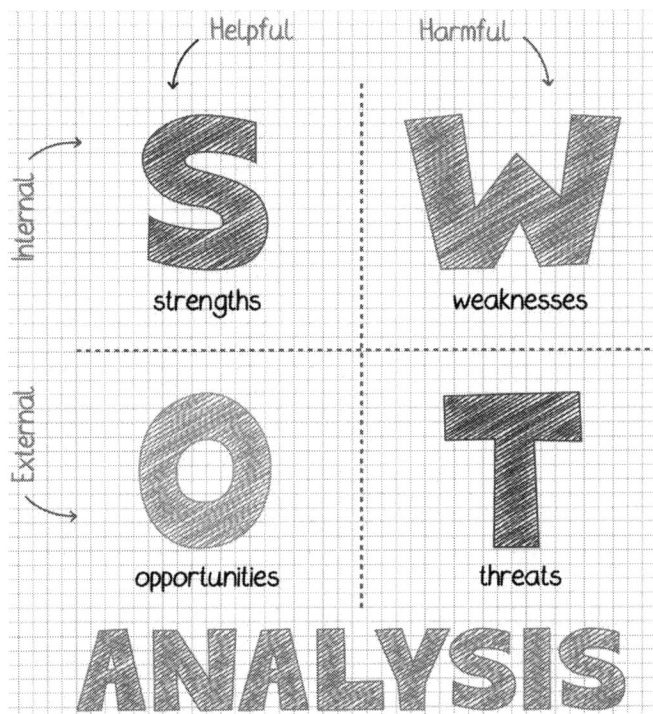

SWOT can be helpful when tackling large projects or relatively simple ones. It is vital that you have a specific question in mind, such as evaluating a new business idea or potential partnership. It will help you unearth weaknesses in a plan or project you might not have otherwise considered. SWOT is useful in the early stages of a project or when you have hit a roadblock. It can also help you evaluate your personal strengths and weaknesses as a business owner.

Take note of the passionate presenters on *Shark Tank* who have borrowed money and invested untold hours into their business, only to get blasted by the Sharks with questions that they had not considered. Raw emotion and passion can drive you, but without a plan, you could waste valuable time and resources. Starting and running your business without a plan is like departing on a journey without a map or GPS. You will be wandering from one place to another and possibly driving many miles in the wrong direction. Without a strategic plan, it will be impossible for you to hear that lady screaming, "Recalculating!" and "Take a U turn at the next intersection!"

This mission of this entire book has been to ask yourself the right questions to have the life and business you want. That is the job of a strategic plan in its simplest form.

Passion is a key ingredient and essential fuel to move you forward, but it must be accompanied by a plan that is logical and simple. It must be logical because it needs to make sense in the real world and simple because if it is too complicated you will procrastinate and never execute the steps required.

Creating a strategic business plan can be a daunting task, but the effort will help you define your goals and provide clear direction. It will also expose your weaknesses and help you avoid setbacks that can stifle your growth.

Dan Miller said, "If you can't see your business on paper, you will never see it in reality."[4]

CHAPTER 11

Bonus Question: "Should Your Business Give Back?"

I love *Shark Tank* updates. It's exciting to see the progress a business has made since they first appeared on the show. Many of the updates have one thing in common: they make it their mission to give back. These businesses have decided to take a portion of their success and give back to their community or a particular organization that has special meaning to them.

In season 5, Rick and Melissa Hinnant entered *Shark Tank* to pitch their business, Grace and Lace. After some intense negotiation, they settled on a deal with Barbara Corcoran. According to their recent appearance on *Beyond the Tank*, their gross sales have exceeded $12 million and have made them one of Barbara's most profitable businesses. In 2010, the business was born out of the tragic loss of their child. Melissa began sewing while in the hospital, and the rest is history. Rick and Melissa give a portion of every sale to *Angel House*, which builds orphanages in India. They built two orphanages in 2014 and five more in 2015 that house fifty orphans each.

> *We make a living by what we get. We make a life by what we give.*[1]
> —WINSTON CHURCHILL

In season 6, cofounders Anna Stork and Andrea Sreshta pitched their product Lumin-Aid and inked a deal with Mark Cuban. LuminAid is a solar-powered inflatable lantern that is compact, waterproof, and rechargeable. It was designed to help post-earthquake efforts in Haiti. Their product is being used in over seventy countries and for disaster relief around the world. They have given away thousands of lights through their various charitable projects.

Fleetwood Hicks found a unique way to give back by creating *Villy Custom Remarkable Ride Foundation,* which allows kids battling cancer to design and receive their own custom *dream* bike. Hicks wanted to honor his mother, who lost her battle with cancer in 2005. He said, "I remember my mom saying not to feel sorry for her—to feel sorry for the kids going through something so awful as a child."

One of the most inspirational presentations came from Johnny George's Tree-T-Pee. It's a device that helps farmers save water in the irrigation of plants and trees. Guest Shark John Paul De Joria saw the vision and invested, allowing Tree-T-Pee to help farmers all across the country and securing a deal with Home Depot. George's story about working alongside his father was inspirational, along with his personal passion to help fellow farmers.

Stella Valle, a Lori Greiner investment, decided to help the military organization *Team Red, White, and Blue*. Robert

Bonus Question: "Should Your Business Give Back?"

Herjavac's investment Tipsy Elves gives sweaters to children in need. Drop Stop donated their product to their local police department to set the example for safe driving.

There are many good reasons to make giving back part of your company's mission. One advantage is that it creates good PR. A study by Cone Communications in 2013 stated that 91 percent of global consumers are likely to switch brands to one associated with a good cause given comparable price and quality.[2] The Reputation Institute published a study that states 59 percent of consumers would go out of their way to communicate something positive about companies they see as being good corporate citizens.[3]

> *I fully believe that God has given me this business as a platform—a platform to inspire others to dream big and beyond their wildest imagination.*
> —RICK AND MELISSA HINNANT

Companies that give back have improved employee morale. Employee engagement studies show a spike to 68 percent when employees had positive feelings toward the company's commitment. The Corporate Leadership Council found that employees who are most committed perform 20 percent better and are 87 percent less likely to leave your organization.

Kevin O'Leary said, "The DNA of a business is to make money for its shareholders, not to solve all the problems of society."[4] Lori Greiner says, "I'm the opposite of Kevin. It's not all about the money. It's about doing good, giving back and helping others."

I agree with Kevin O'Leary about profitability. You cannot give back if you are not making money. The good will of your company should come from your surplus. However, what you do with those profits is a different issue entirely.

Generosity is a natural progression of gratitude. Studies show that if you have an attitude of thankfulness, you will be more willing to do something for someone else. Besides, giving back just feels good.[5]

> *If someone has a great generosity of spirit, it multiplies. They always make money. It's just the way it is.*
> —BARBARA CORCORAN

CHAPTER 12

Summary

Entrepreneurship is a dream for many people. *Shark Tank* reminds viewers that there are people right at this moment acting on the spark of an idea, creating a plan, and generating sales. The message is loud and clear. The American Dream is available to everyone.

For many, *Shark Tank* has become a family event, with their children enjoying the show as much as adults. Robert Herjavec mentioned in a recent episode that 50 percent of fans who approach him are young people.

Regardless of our age, the show has allowed us to peek behind the curtain to see real presentations and live negotiations. We have witnessed millionaires being created right before our eyes. We have watched as cold-blooded Sharks shed tears as they hear a story of sacrifice and loss.

My podcast has always been about gleaning knowledge from the millionaires and billionaires who sit on the panel. The Sharks have different backgrounds and approaches to the process. All of them are self-made. They all started with very little, worked hard, and made it happen. I find that refreshing. That means the same opportunity is available for any of us if we are willing to learn and pay the price.

The title of this book asks a challenging question: "Could You Survive *Shark Tank*?" If pursuing an opportunity to pitch to the Sharks is your goal, I hope you achieve it. As I mentioned earlier in this book, there are times we do not know the right questions to ask. However, if you can answer the questions outlined in this book, I believe you are well on your way to owning a successful business and surviving any *Shark Tank* you choose to swim in.

> *Success and significance cannot be defined universally. We're human, so we have the ability to choose what we deem to be "success" for us individually.*
> —AARON WALKER,
> *View from the Top*[1]

One last thought...

In your pursuit of success in any way you choose to define it, my hope is that you do not lose focus on what is most important. I do not believe you have to sacrifice your faith, family, relationships and health to be successful. Any worthy goal requires sacrifice but be cognizant of each decision and create a strategic plan that will help you create the life you want.

My dream is that you not only succeed in business but succeed in creating your best life.

Your Next Step:

Congratulations on finishing the first step! Now you know the *Right* questions to ask.

Do you believe you could survive *Shark Tank*? I recommend you stop and complete the *Surviving Shark Tank* assessment at **piercemarrs.com/assessment**. It's quick, easy, and essential to get a baseline of your current business. Don't beat yourself up if you do not have all the answers. That's why you bought this book, right? If you do have all the answers, you are already on your way to a successful, thriving business. Consider this a great opportunity to give your business a checkup to help you stay on track.

After you complete the assessment, I have provided a number of tools and resources to help you on your journey of building a successful business. You can find them at

piercemarrs.com/resources

Acknowledgments

I am blessed to be surrounded by family and friends who are supportive and encouraging. Thank you all for your presence in my life.

To Lesa, my wife and best friend. You have been a constant source of encouragement and unwavering support in my life for over thirty-five years. I am grateful beyond words. Thank you for your patience and support while it took way too long to complete this manuscript.

To Steve Hayes, my friend of over forty years. If you had not agreed to co-host and bring your insight and humor to the *Shark Tank Fan Podcast* nine years ago, this book would have never happened. I owe you a huge thanks.

To Jimi Gibson, my friend and accountability partner. Thank you for patiently walking through this process with me and sharing your branding expertise in this book.

To Dan Miller, my friend and mentor. I will be forever grateful for our divine meeting on a train one rainy night many years ago. It changed the direction of my life. Thank you for being a dreamer and helping me believe.

To Deb Ingino, my soul sister. You are a priceless friend in so many ways. Thank you for co-hosting the podcast and sharing your wisdom in this book.

To Aaron Krause, Kent Julian, and Emily Chase Smith, thank you for your invaluable contribution to this book.

To Mark Burnett and the producers of *Shark Tank*, thank you for inspiring people of all ages to keep the dream of entrepreneurship alive and well.

Last, but not least, I want to thank all of the entrepreneurs who joined me on the podcast to share their journey and wisdom.

Dorothy Parker and several other accomplished authors have stated in some form or other, "I hate writing, I love having written." I understand what they mean. Writing is an arduous task. However, for me, writing was easier than finishing. I had to remind myself many times, "The best is the enemy of the good." I believe this is good.

Notes

Chapter 1

1. Merriam-Webster.com, s.v. "entrepreneur," https://www.merriam-webster.com/dictionary/entrepreneur.

2. US Small Business Administration Office of Advocacy: 2019 Small Business Profile; https://cdn.advocacy.sba.gov/wp-content/uploads/2019/04/23142610/2019-Small-Business-Profiles-States-Territories.pdf.

3. *Shark Tank*, Season 11, Episode 2, aired October 6th, 2019 on ABC.

Chapter 3

1. Godin, Seth "The Hard Parts," Seth's Blog, April 28th, 2013; https://seths.blog/2013/04/the-hard-parts/.

2. "Elon Musk on the 1 Creative Skill Every Founder Needs Now" by Lisa Calhoun, *Inc.* Magazine, Published March 15th, 2017, https://www.inc.com/lisa-calhoun/elon-musk-on-the-1-creative-skill-every-founder-needs-now.html.

3. Michael E. Gerber, *The E-Myth Revisited: Why Most Small Business Don't Work and What to Do About It*, Harper Business; Updated, October 14, 2004.

Chapter 4

1. "Mark Cuban's Top 3 Rules for Business Success… and 1 Secret" by Kimberly Weisul, Inc.com, Published May 20, 2015, https://www.inc.com/kimberly-weisul/mark-cuban-three-rules-business-success-one-secret.html.

2. Merriam-Webster.com, s.v. "viable," https://www.merriam-webster.com/dictionary/viable.

3. Dictionary.com, Necessity is the mother of invention, by the ancient Greek philosopher Plato, This saying appears in the dialogue Republic, https://www.dictionary.com/browse/necessity-is-the-mother-of-invention.

4. "7 Things You Should Know About Life and Money According to *Shark Tank*'s Kevin O'Leary" by Ken Sterling, Inc.com quote: "If you aren't making money after three years, you have a hobby—not a business," Published June 10, 2019, https://www.inc.com/ken-sterling/7-things-you-should-know-about-life-money-according-to-shark-tanks-kevin-oleary.html.

5. APPA, American Pet Products, Pet Industry Market Size & Ownership Statistics. In 2018, $72.56 billion was spent on our pets in the U.S., https://www.americanpetproducts.org/press_industrytrends.asp.

6. Wikipedia, s.v. "niche market," https://en.wikipedia.org/wiki/Niche_market.

7. CNBC.com, "Mark Cuban reveals 3 secrets for growing a successful business," by Catherine Clifford, "There has never been a company in the history of companies that has ever succeeded without sales," https://www.cnbc.com/2018/02/09/

mark-cuban-reveals-3-secrets-for-growing-a-successful-business.html.

8. Parade.com, "*Shark Tank*'s Kevin O'Leary; 'You've Got to Know the Numbers—Or I Will Eviscerate You,' " https://parade.com/270623/jasonlynch/shark-tanks-kevin-oleary-youve-got-to-know-the-numbers-or-i-will-eviscerate-you/.

9. Self Made, https://self-made.io/6-famous-people-who-lost-all-their-money/1360/3/.

10. Huff Post.com, http://www.huffingtonpost.com/2011/12/12/mc-hammer-sued-by-us-gove_n_1143853.html.

11. CNN Business, http://money.cnn.com/2014/12/02/luxury/richest-recording-artists/.

Chapter 5

1. Investopedia.com, s.v. "valuation," https://www.investopedia.com/terms/v/valuation.asp.

2. Brainy Quote, Kevin Harrington quote, "Nothing turns off an investor more than when an entrepreneur comes in with a ridiculous valuatio," https://www.brainyquote.com/quotes/kevin_harrington_433448.

3. *Success* Magazine, "Shark Attack" by Shelley Levitt, Lori Greiner quote, October 2015 Issue, pg 45.

4. Business Insider, Barbara Corcoran: Being Too Passionate is Bad for Business by Jenna Goudreau, https://www.businessinsider.com/barbara-corcoran-being-too-passionate-is-bad-for-business-2014-4, April 23, 2014.

5. *Success* Magazine, "Swimming Lessons" by Shelley Levitt, Mark Cuban quote, March 2018 Issue, pg 38.

Chapter 6

1. *The Power of Broke: How Empty Pockets, a Tight Budget, and a Hunger for Success Can Become Your Greatest Advantage* by Daymond John, Published by Currency, January 19, 2016.

2. SmallBizTrends.com, "Startup Statistics—The Numbers You Need to Know" by Matt Mansfield, Published March 28, 2019.

3. Wikipedia, s.v. "crowdfunding," https://en.wikipedia.org/wiki/Crowdfunding.

4. *Chicken Soup for the Soul* series, https://www.chickensoup.com/.

Chapter 7

1. BusinessInsider.com, "'Shark Tank' Investor Lori Greiner explains the 7 Things She Looks for in a Pitch" by Richard Feloni, Published March 16, 2016, https://www.businessinsider.com/shark-tank-lori-greiner-explains-perfect-pitch-2016-3.

Chapter 9

1. SmallBizTrends.com, https://smallbiztrends.com/2019/03/startup-statistics-small-business.html.

Chapter 10

1. Medium.com, Warren Buffet quote, https://medium.com/azoth/be-productive-in-your-sleep-warren-buffett-wisdom-on-idiots-24c34e9036a8.

2. BusinessDictionary.com, s.v. "distribution channel," http://www.businessdictionary.com/definition/distribution-channel.html.

3. Brainy Quote, Picasso quote, https://www.brainyquote.com/quotes/pablo_picasso_120939.

4. Dan Miller quote, https://www.48days.com/.

Chapter 11

1. Brainy Quote, Winston Churchill quote, https://www.brainyquote.com/quotes/winston_churchill_131192.

2. Cone Communications Study, https://www.conecomm.com/news-blog/2013-global-csr-study-release.

3. Forbes.com, Reputation Institute Study, https://www.forbes.com/sites/brucerogers/2013/10/07/too-many-feelings-and-not-enough-facts-in-csr-strategy/#509b532160cf.

4. Kevin O'Leary DNA quote, https://miamiherald.typepad.com/the-starting-gate/2014/11/kevin-oleary-aka-mr-wonderful.html.

5. https://abcnews.go.com/Business/.

Chapter 12

1. Walker, Aaron, *View from the Top: Living a Life of Significance*, Published by Morgan James, 2017, pg 179, https://www.viewfromthetop.com/book.

About the Author

Pierce Marrs, President of Marrs Coaching, is a coach, speaker, writer and podcaster. He believes that communication is key and specializes in helping individuals and teams understand their own wiring and how to communicate effectively with others. With thirty-five years experience as a sales professional, Pierce brings a wealth of knowledge to the table along with multiple certifications in DISC Personality Assessments and Coaching. He is an avid blogger and served as host and producer of the popular *Shark Tank Fan Podcast* since 2011. Pierce believes that empathy and effective communication can be a game changer in building strong personal and professional relationships.

Learn more about Pierce at http://www.piercemarrs.com/

Made in the USA
Middletown, DE
21 March 2020